GENERAL LEARNING OBJECTIVES OF

This Open Learning Unit will supply you with the core information you need to answer examination questions on the theoretical basis of developmental psychology and the methods required for studying change. It will also equip you with sufficient detail to write an essay on play or moral development. It will take you 3 or 4 hours to work through, although if you attempt all the suggested activities it will take longer.

As this is the core Open Learning Unit in the series on developmental psychology you may find it useful to re-examine sections of it when studying other topics or reading the other Units.

By the end of this Unit you should understand:

▷ the philosophical, biological, social policy and cultural issues which form the basis of developmental psychology;

▷ the methods we use to study how individuals <u>change</u> at key points in development;

▷ the nature of play and how ideas within the biological sciences influence our understanding of the topic;

▷ the stage-like developments in children's understanding of morality.

Developmental Psychology: the study of change

If you reflect back over the course of your life you may remember times and events when you thought and acted in ways which were radically different to now. People change over time. Developmental psychology is concerned with how we *change* and what causes those changes. **Physiological** change is easy to demonstrate. Our bodies grow and their functions alter; for example, infants gain the ability to walk and adolescents become able to reproduce. Experience in crawling or in a 'baby walker' may advance the onset of walking, but only by a few weeks; walking is a feature of maturation that is genetically programmed within us. Physical changes are accompanied and paralleled by psychological ones. We become more able to think in complex ways. Our emotions and relationships change as we mature.

You will have noticed that I have used the word 'change' a lot. The key question for developmental psychology is how does this change occur – how does one psychological process transform itself into another? How, for example, do we gain the ability to engage in more complex interaction? The aim of this Unit is to explore some of the core issues so that you can address these questions. First some theoretical background is required.

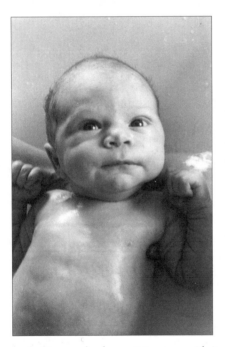 

FIGURE 1. *Human development is very rapid: in only a few years the child is transformed from an infant to an active member of society.*

Before we start, write a few notes about how you think psychological changes might occur - -what causes us to act, think and feel differently over the course of life? You can compare these notes with the discussion in Part 2.

155.2

(HHC)

CONTENTS

1

Theoretical Connections

KEY AIMS: By reading this Part you should know how current discussion within developmental psychology stems from debates over four issues:

▷ philosophical concerns over the relative contributions of inherited and learned ways of acting (the nature/nurture controversy)

▷ evolutionary biology: the study of developments within and across species

▷ social issues which influence the way we perceive the process of development

▷ the role of culture in development.

Like psychology as a whole, developmental psychology is a young science; yet it addresses questions which have been asked by other disciplines over a long time period. Figure 2 shows the major connections between developmental psychology and related fields of study. We shall reflect on each of these links in turn.

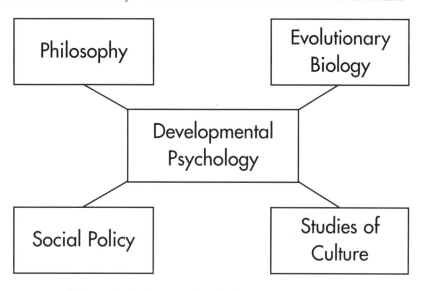

FIGURE 2: *Major links within developmental psychology.*

Philosophy and Developmental Psychology

For over three thousand years philosophers have argued about what it is to be human. In particular, there are two important philosophical questions. The first concerns *our abilities to perceive and to think.* How do we make sense of the light that hits the retina in the back of the eye or the sound that vibrates our ear-drums? How, indeed, are we able to reflect upon what we see, hear and know? What is meant by consciousness? The Unit, *Perception,* explores these issues in detail. For our purposes such questions naturally give rise to further questions about *the origins of such capabilities,* which is the second issue of concern to developmental psychologists. Philosophers and scholars of religion couch their questions rather differently – are people born with 'original sin' as the Bible suggests, or are they born innocent and 'corrupted' by the world in which they live?

The same question would be expressed differently in developmental psychological terms. On the one hand, the issue of original sin versus innocence is seen in the questions raised about to what extent our make-up is determined by inborn abilities. This is the so-called **innate**, **nativist** or **nature** argument. On the other hand, opponents of the innate view of development have long argued that we are moulded by our environments – particularly by the way in which others treat us. This is the **empiricist** or **nurture** perspective. In all the units which accompany this one you will find that the nature/nurture controversy has dominated discussion of children's capabilities and is still influential. The debate still continues particularly in areas such as the psychological differences betwen males and females (see the Unit on *Sex, Gender and Identity* by Patricia Turner). However, nowadays most developmental psychologists concentrate on investigating how inborn or genetic influences combine with stimulation from the environment to produce changes in the child's development.

SAQ
1

In the nature versus nurture debate, on which side would you put the following statements?
'Boys will be boys'
'Some leaders are born great'
'I'm depraved on account of being deprived'
'Some leaders have greatness thrust upon them'
'Ryan Giggs is an instinctive footballer'.

Evolutionary biology and developmental psychology

The nature/nurture debate within philosophy tended to concern theological or educational issues – for example whether children should be taught by a harsh regime to quell their natural instincts or whether we should teach them mainly by encouragement and good example. However, the debate changed and intensified in the nineteenth century with the publication in 1859 of Charles Darwin's *The Origin of Species*. More coherently than anyone before, Darwin argued that the human species evolved from its biological relatives, the great apes. While ridiculed by leading churchmen of the day – about whether they were descended from a chimpanzee on their mother's or father's side of the family! – Darwin and his followers had two profound influences upon 'developmental science'.

FIGURE 3: (a) *Wide-open mouth laughter by a human infant in a tickling game. The wide-open mouth version without retracted lips becomes rare in adulthood.*

(b) *Relaxed open-mouth face in a capucin monkey, while being tickled by a human being.*

The first influence was, of course, the establishment of evolutionary biology as a field of study, leading to the discovery of DNA and the study of genetics in the twentieth century. It also focused debate on the question of the differences and similarities between ourselves and the great apes. What distinguishes us from them? Are we simply more skilled or do we have capabilities which set us aside from our near relatives? Such questions are investigated by developmental psychologists in studies in which the capabilities of apes and people are closely compared, and also in examination of children's development.

Secondly, Darwin's work established developmental research as a scientific endeavour. He observed closely the natural selection of species such as those in the Galapagos Islands off the mainland coast of Ecuador. In his meticulous record keeping and theoretical insights he showed the scientific world the power of observation. He carried on this work by detailing the early development of his son (nicknamed 'Doddy') which he completed in the 1870s. In this study Darwin attempted not only to reveal the close links between the species but he also signalled the beginnings of meticulous research on early child development as a worthwhile enterprise.

SAQ
2

In what two ways did Darwin's work influence the way in which children were studied?

Social policy influences on developmental psychology

It would be wrong to suggest that developmental psychology is concerned only with age-old questions about the nature of perception and thinking and the more recent issue of the place of *homo sapiens* in the evolutionary chain. The discipline has always been immersed in wider social and political debates (as mentioned earlier) about the appropriate way to bring up our young and, more usually, attempts to solve social problems involving children. Around the time of Darwin's study of his son the topic of children's development and education was being debated widely both in political circles and in the press. There were, for example, two major education acts in Britain during the 1870s establishing some schooling for all children. The reason for this interest in children's welfare stemmed in part from a heightened concern with the effects of social change – industrialization of manufacturing – upon family life. With their parents at work for most of the day the presence of unsupervised children on the streets presented a serious problem of social order. *Oliver Twist* by Charles Dickens provides an excellent, if fictitious, example of this.

An analysis of any historical period shows just how interlinked are pressing social issues and the ideas raised by developmental psychologists. In many respects their work reflects the prevailing social attitudes of the day. Compare, for example, the advice given in manuals for parents in the 1920s and in the 1990s. Before the Second World War 'experts' believed that environmental influences exerted a strong influence upon children, so parents were advised to stick to a strict routine. For example, babies should be fed regularly at three- (or perhaps four-) hourly intervals irrespective of whether they cried between feeds. This was the **'hygienist'** approach as it emphasized order and hygiene (or cleanliness). Since the Second World War, child-rearing views have changed, becoming more **permissive**. Child care manuals now suggest that babies should be fed on demand, when their cries suggest they need to suckle. The shift from hygienism to permissiveness came about largely as a result of economic and social changes. Developmental psychology has largely moved with the times rather than having caused such shifts.

SAQ
3

On which sides of the nature/nurture debate are the hygienist and the permissive approaches to child rearing?

The lesson from such social changes is that we should not forget that the ways in which developmental psychologists view children, and the questions asked by research, are strongly influenced by prevailing social practices (like hygienism or permissiveness), and the pressing social problems of the day (such as youth crime in the 1870s). So in the 1980s researchers focused upon issues like the effects of divorce upon children, reflecting a general social concern with the continuing increase in parental separation and the breakdown of traditional values. Research in the 1990s has increasingly studied the effects of remarriage upon children and the dynamics of step-families. There are many other social issues which influence our thinking. Some current examples are: Should children with learning disabilities be taught in special schools or should they be in normal schools so that they are more integrated into the wider society? Do children born very prematurely develop in the same way as full-term babies now that those weighing 1 kilo often survive? How has the spread of AIDS and global political instability influenced the beliefs and values of teenagers and young adults?

SOMETHING TO TRY

Make a list of some of the social issues of today which might influence the way in which we understand development. You might like to do this with friends or classmates so that you can compare notes with them. You need not confine yourself to the period of childhood; developmental change continues throughout life.

Culture and development

The fact that the research of developmental psychologists often reflects social issues of the day suggests something fundamental about the nature of development which is often overlooked: that development is embedded within a social environment. Social policies and ideas influence the theories we construct; so too are children influenced by prevailing beliefs and practices. Many psychologists have attempted to play down the influence of culture on development. This is not surprising for two reasons. First, it is tempting to assume that psychological processes, like perceptions, thoughts and emotions, are what goes on 'in the mind' irrespective of any outside social influences. Secondly, the 'social influences' that constitute cultures are so complex that it seems hard enough to describe them, let alone understand their impact upon the ways we think and act. So traditionally there has been a divide between psychologists, who study what goes on in the mind, and those who investigate social processes (sociologists) and culture (anthropologists).

While these divisions are apparent there have always been attempts to bridge the gaps. For example, anthropologists in the 1920s, like Margaret Mead, described the impact of different cultural settings upon the course of development. A main aim was to show that Western beliefs and findings about growing up may not be shared by non-Western cultures. One of Mead's studies showed that adolescence in the Pacific island of Samoa is a very different and less painful process than it is in the industrial nations. Her book, *Coming of Age in Samoa* (1928) still makes fascinating reading. There are many intriguing cross-cultural comparisons in the literature on human development. The problem is that it is difficult to incorporate them into our theoretical understanding. If we examine the most popular current attempt to fit human development into its social context we shall see some of the difficulties.

In 1979 the leading American developmental psychologist, Urie Bronfenbrenner, described his theory in a book entitled *The Ecology of Human Development*. For Bronfenbrenner, the individual is immersed in a social environment with many different layers. These are illustrated by the concentric circles in Figure 4.

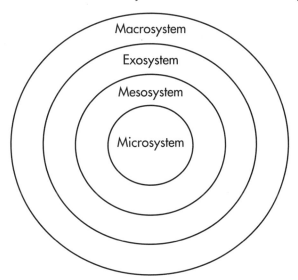

FIGURE 4: *Bronfenbrenner's ecology of human development.*

The **microsystem** represents the individual's interactions with others – for example the child's daily encounters with his or her family, teachers and friends. The **mesosystem** is the part of the social world which links different aspects of the child's daily encounters (in the microsystem) together. For example, if parents help the child with homework the child may well get on better with the teacher. The two outer rings in Figure 4 refer to the wider society. The **exosystem** refers to all those social processes which have an indirect influence on individuals. For example, access to pre-school nurseries may play a part in how parents manage child care and, by implication, their interactions with their children. Such access is strongly influenced by local government policy towards nurseries.

FIGURE5: *Schooling is one cultural influence on development.*

Finally, the **macrosystem** refers to the wider belief system of the particular culture. We have considered some of these with reference to hygienism and permissiveness in the previous section. The Israeli kibbutz system is another good example of a macrosystem which differs from our own. Children are reared, at least some of the time, in nurseries by specially trained carers called 'metapelot'. Such arrangements are established to emphasize the importance of the social group as well as the family.

Bronfenbrenner describes how each of these systems fits around the individual like a set of Russian dolls – one inside the other. This description is useful but if you picture a set of dolls, one inside the other, you will see that there are no connections between the different layers (the dolls, in this case). In the same way, Bronfenbrenner's model serves only as a description of some of the richness of the patterns of influences on our life; it does not show *how* the parts fit together, nor the relative contribution of each part.

SAQ
4

Describe briefly the four layers of Bronfenbrenner's model. What are its major strengths and weaknesses?

Summary

- ❑ Developmental psychology addresses issues raised in discussion on four topics: philosophy, evolutionary biology, social policy and culture.

- ❑ The effects of nature and nurture combine to produce the course of human development.

- ❑ Evolutionary biology has taught us to examine the skills which distinguish us from other species and has provided us with observational methods for doing so.

- ❑ Social issues of the day, like the effects of divorce on families, greatly influence how we regard development.

- ❑ Human development is guided by a range of influences, from individual relationships to much wider social and cultural processes.

Ontogeny: The Development of the Individual

KEY AIMS: By reading this Part you should:

▷   consider whether development is marked by gradual, continuous, change or by rapid or discontinuous shifts in understanding

▷   understand that development involves two factors, the genotype (the individual's genetic inheritance) and the environment

▷   be able to distinguish three theoretical perceptions on the gene-environment relationship: social learning, maturation and constructivism.

Look back at Figure 2. This shows that developmental psychology draws from diverse traditions of thinking about the nature of human development. In this Part we will explore the issues that modern developmental theory considers to be central. It is fair to suggest that all the big questions asked and the major theories hinge upon the relative contributions of nature and of nurture to development . In this section we will explore the various perspectives on **ontogeny** – the development of an individual member of a species. Part 3 examines human development in terms of **phylogeny** – the evolutionary development of the species. But first it is important to consider another issue that cuts across the issues discussed in the nature/nurture debate. This is the issue of *how* development occurs; the question of whether development is smooth and continuous or discontinuous occurring in separate, distinct stages.

Continuity or Discontinuity?

In nature there are two ways in which organisms grow. The first involves simple expansion while the other is more complex. Look at Figure 6; this shows the life-course of two distinct creatures, a coral and a butterfly. Coral is not alive, of course, but it will serve as an example to demonstrate a point.

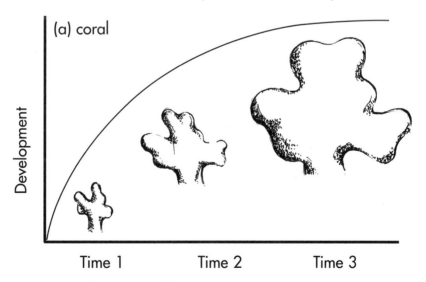

FIGURE 6(a): *Development of coral.*

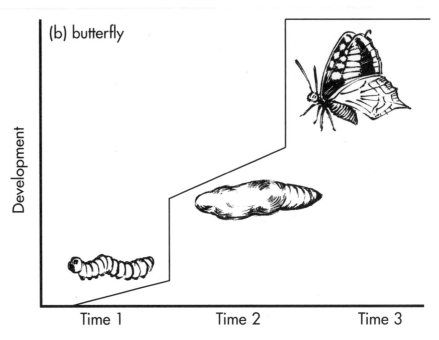

FIGURE 6(a): *Development of butterfly*

Look first at the growth of the coral. At each of the three time periods shown in Figure 6(a) the basic structure remains the same. The polyps build on the existing structure without changing what has been added before. The shape might alter but only as a result of additions to the structure. The development is therefore **linear**, or continuous, as shown by the line in part (a) of Figure 6. It is curved because I assume that less growth occurs as the coral matures. If you plotted your height from birth to the present day on a graph like this it would flatten out in the same way after the growth spurt of adolescence. It is important to note that most developmental psychologists would use·the term 'growth' to describe such change, not the term 'development', as they believe that the life-course is marked by more dramatic, qualitative shifts in understanding and action.

Compare the life-course of coral with the life-course of the butterfly. In the latter case, two dramatic changes occur in both structure and function. A caterpillar (time 1) may grow in a linear way by shedding its outer layers but, somewhat suddenly, it transforms into a pupa. The time 3 shift is even more dramatic – when the fully grown butterfly emerges. Of course, development is occurring all the time, but at certain points changes in the function of the organism, like the onset of the ability to fly, are sudden and irreversible. This developmental progression is characterized by the steps or stages outlined in part (b) of Figure 6. Most developmental psychologists believe that human intellectual growth proceeds in this **stage-like** way. People, especially young children, show dramatic changes and transformations which are equally as exciting as those of the butterfly. Theoreticians like Sigmund Freud, who examined the individual's development of sexual identity resulting from biological maturation, and Jean Piaget, who focused primarily on the child's intellectual capabilities, put heavy emphasis on stage- or step-like transitions in development. (The companion Unit *Cognitive and Language Development* describes Piaget's theory, while the Unit *Early Socialization* discusses the influence of Freud's theory on recent ideas.)

So what are the characteristics of these stages? Developmentalists point to four defining features:

1. **Holism**: any one area of intellectual functioning is related to the others. So, for example, when children acquire new cognitive abilities in the primary school years, such as learning to read or understand simple mathematics, they also become able to engage in more complex patterns of friendship and play. In the primary school years children also become interested in games with rules (like playground fantasy games). These games require greater levels of intellectual skill. At the same time such activities change the nature of children's relationships, so that a group identity emerges in a class.

2. **Simultaneity** : Since different aspects of psychological functioning relate to one another, when changes occur in one area they tend to effect shifts in others.

3. **Rapidity** : Like the butterfly emerging from the pupa's shell, change is thought to be very rapid. The vertical rise of the steps in Figure 6(b) illustrates this.

4. **Qualitative change** : Once the transition has occurred the individual becomes a different person. Not only does he or she use a newly acquired skill but this makes them think and act in different ways.

SAQ
5

Outline two critical differences between views of development based upon continuity and those based on discontinuity.

This concept of 'stage' is a key one in developmental psychology. To consider what this implies think back to some earlier period in your life that you can remember well – your first years at school, for example. Did you think about and see your family or friendships in similar or different ways to now? Stage theorists would argue that how you perceive the world now is radically different from your earlier perceptions and thoughts. Have you ever wondered why most people can remember little, if anything, of their first five years? One possible reason is that our understanding of the world now is so different that we cannot bring to mind the very different ideas and images we had at that time.

SOMETHING TO TRY
Ask your friends and family what they can remember of their own first five years, and then a second question, 'Are you sure you remember this or are you simply repeating what you have been told happened?'

Genotype and the environment

The biological building blocks of development are the pairs of chromosomes (one from each parent) present in every cell (excluding the reproductive cells) of an organism. The complete 'package' of genetic information stored on the chromosomes is called the **genotype**. This establishes the constraints and possibilities for development. In response to the conundrums raised in earlier philosophical debates about nature and

FIGURE 7: *Babies remember little of their early life and rely on parents to recall it for them.*

nurture, biologists in the twentieth century have come largely to agree that development is produced as a result of the *interaction* between the genotype and the environment. By the term interaction they mean that each component part is necessary and they combine together to produce both physical and psychological changes. The basis of this process is shown in Figure 4. But the nature/nurture argument is not dead. As we shall see, theories of development still differ fundamentally on the relative importance they place on either the environment or the genotype in the equation.

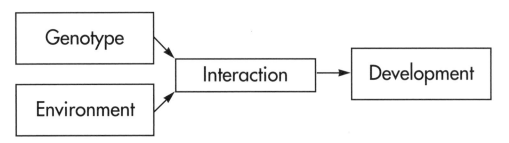

FIGURE 8: A *biological model of development.*

Before we consider three variations on the model in Figure 8, let us examine a few examples from biology to show the possible variations. In the 1930s biologists coined the term **'instinct'** to describe behaviours that are driven solely by our genetic make-up. The term is now widely used. Football commentators, for example, often describe a striker's goal-scoring abilities as 'instinctive', as if his skills were inborn. However, there is no evidence to show the primacy of genetics over environmental influences behind such abilities. Biologists have realized that the concept of instinct is very complex. Let's look at the example of bird-song. At one extreme there are birds like the cuckoo which are raised by foster-parents – their eggs are laid in other birds' nests and the parents have no contact with their offspring. Cuckoos develop their familiar song nevertheless, so it must be instinctive. At the other extreme, experiments have shown that bullfinches raised with canaries develop the foster-parents' song, not their own, so their song is learned rather than instinctive. The chaffinch occupies a place in the middle of this continuum. When raised in isolation from other chaffinches, but with birds of different species, chaffinches develop some song but not the full and lyrical chorus of their relatives throughout the world. Thus there is something about chaffinch 'culture' that must be learned and passed on from one generation to the next.

What do the examples of bird-song tell us about the nature of instinctive capability? They show differences between species; that in some respects environmental pulls may be stronger (e.g. the bullfinch), while in others the genotype needs little external triggering to operate successfully (e.g. the cuckoo). So, where does human behaviour fit on this continuum? As you might expect the answer is far from simple and varies according to which aspect of psychological functioning is looked at; nor is the question settled. There are three main theoretical positions, at which we will now look.

1. Environmental influences: the social learning perspective

Learning Theory, an earlier and more extreme version of this view, supported the nurture (or empiricist) argument. This played down any possible influences of the genotype and claimed that all development can be attributed to the modifications on the organism caused by environmental rewards and punishments. Influential figures such as B.F. Skinner believed that just as you can 'shape' a pigeon's behaviour so that it will peck on a bar to receive a reward of food, so too you can socialize children into becoming good or bad citizens. To some extent the scientific aims of the learning theorists or behaviourists drove the theory; since we cannot directly perceive and measure people's thoughts and feelings, they argued that we cannot study them directly – we can only assess behaviour. It is true that the individual's perception of the environment is hard to discern (an issue we shall return to later) but most learning theorists have been forced to admit that the impact of the genotype-environment interaction cannot be ignored.

The modified environmental approach is known as the social learning theory. Both biological and interactional factors are taken into account in this theory, in that the organism is thought to be predisposed to be rewarded for imitating important figures like parents, peer- group leaders and television personalities. However, social learning theorists still argue that environmental rewards are the key to understanding development and play the major part. Figure 5 indicates this relative weighting by the different sizes of the boxes.

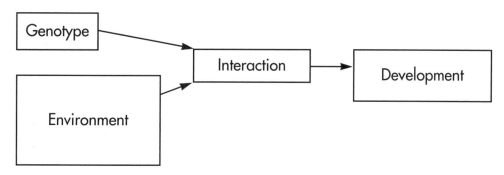

FIGURE 9: *The social learning perspective*.

What aspects of development might the social learning perspective help us explain? Proponents of this viewpoint underline just how much children will imitate so-called **'role models'**. The most famous experiments concern children's imitation of aggressive actors. Albert Bandura (1971), the major figure in this field, set up a series of studies in which children witnessed an adult being violent, either in person or on television. He then showed that the children tended to copy such acts immediately afterwards.

Social learning theory has also been used to explain the relationship between the style of parenting used and its effects on the child's development. For example, Diana Baumrind (1971) distinguishes between **authoritative** parents, who explain their actions to the child and reward appropriate actions, and **authoritarian** parents, who are inflexible and disciplinarian. Research has repeatedly shown that the children of authoritarian parents display more behaviour problems, such as delinquency.

Social learning accounts of development have been widely used in the USA and were popular in the 1960s and 1970s. But they have their critics. For a start, the experiments in which children copy an aggressive act might not generalize to real life. Many studies on the effects of television have failed to show that violence on television promotes aggression in children, even though many people still hold the belief that it does. Television may make some children copy acts of violence, but only those who are already likely to commit acts of aggression (Liebert and Sprafkin, 1988).

Secondly, by relatively neglecting the roles of the genotype and the genotype-environment interaction, social learning theory cannot fully explain the process of psychological change. It is an account of how social influences might work, rather than an overall theory of development, and therefore addresses a restricted range of questions. These largely concern how individuals acquire social conventions, but even here it leaves much to be explained. For example, the distinction between authoritarian and authoritative parenting styles begs a number of questions about the appropriateness of such labels. Do parents always adopt one style or the other? And why might a parent want to be authoritarian?

Learning theory and social learning theory came from the USA. Can you think of reasons why this might be the case?

There are two conclusions we can draw from social learning approaches to development. The first is that environmental influences might be large when it comes to some aspects of human development, particularly some social conventions such as the amount of respect shown to adults in a particular culture. Second, it is worth noting that learning theory has contributed greatly to our understanding of how clinical psychologists can effectively treat problems developed in childhood. By measuring different interactional styles in minute detail they have helped teachers to establish more productive regimes (for instance, by instigating more rewards than punishments) and have helped clinical psychologists to treat behaviour problems in a system of step-by-step changes in patients' acts. This is known as **behaviour modification**.

SAQ
6

Look back at Figure 6. Does the social learning approach assume that continuity or discontinuity characterizes development?

2. Maturation

Why do most infants become able to walk just after their first birthday? Why do most children begin to talk suddenly and dramatically sometime around their second birthday? Why, at around puberty, do young people develop different interests and friendship patterns? These sorts of questions have been asked by proponents of a set of theories that focus largely upon the individual's biological or innate make-up. They are called maturational because they assume that the environmental triggering of such skills is by no means as important as the genotype which programmes each skill to mature at more or less a particular stage in the life-course. Figure 10 shows this relative importance.

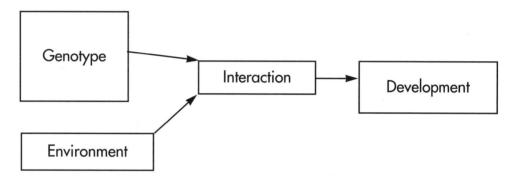

FIGURE 10: *The maturational perspective.*

What are the key features of the maturational perspective?

- The first is that development consists of a set of species-specific patterns of behavioural traits which require minimal prompting to be triggered by the environment.
- The second is that psychological 'maturation' is closely linked with, and often caused by, biological changes. So, teenagers stick posters of sexually attractive people or role models of the same sex on their bedroom walls because their interest is driven by the changes in their bodies prompted by puberty.
- The third is that such changes show a stage-like progression. As biological development occurs in a fixed sequence, so too do our views of the world.

Thus, in many respects, for these theoreticians, our biology is our destiny.

How do the different aspects of development fit together? Does an advance in one area, such as learning to walk, effect change in other aspects of development, like relationships with other children? Theoreticians in this area are divided over this issue. Some argue that maturational changes necessarily cause general changes in the individual's psychological make-up. So, for example, the psychological changes around puberty might be linked with a range of issues. The physiological changes (in brain functioning) account for at least some of the teenager's increased intellectual skills. Other changes in relationships are also evident as a result of puberty, including a renegotiation of roles within the family – being less dependent on parents, for example. It is often assumed that all these changes have the same, largely maturational, trigger.

Others argue that there is relative independence between different areas of psychological functioning. Features like temperament, intelligence or personality have long been thought to be determined largely by genes and to be relatively independent of one another. Each presupposes that there is a strong and lasting effect of the genotype on our capabilities. Throughout this century there have been fierce battles over the evidence for and against these concepts. In the 1950s, for example, intelligence tests were used to select 11-year-olds for grammar schools. However in the 1960s these tests were abandoned in most educational districts because the tests were shown to favour children from middle-class families, who were more familiar with the style of language used in tests. The issue of selection and schooling remains controversial so I will move on to another, less contentious, area of research – language development.

Language: a feature of maturation? Since the 1950s, attention has been paid to how children come to learn language so fast. Individual case studies (e.g. Brown, 1973) have shown that from around the child's second birthday the spoken vocabulary increases from about 100 or 200 to around 2000 words. Figure 7 gives some example of these growth spurts in children's language development.

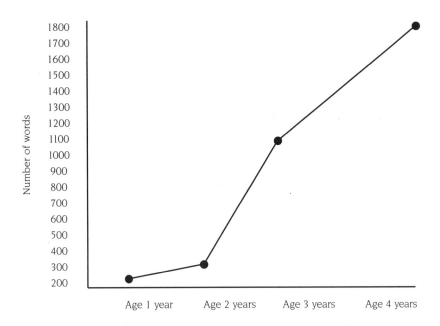

FIGURE 11: *Words understood by the child over the first four years.*

Figure 7 shows that the emergence of spoken language is rapid and dramatic. What causes this 'spurt' at age 2? Young children might be very fast learners but this development cannot simply be explained by coaching. Nor is it likely that toddlers are reluctant to use words until they are really sure of their meaning; there is a lot of experimenting with words. The best explanation is that there is a particular intellectual capability (probably a series of neural circuits in the brain) which suddenly becomes active at about two years of age. Moreover, as the linguist Noam Chomsky (1957) pointed out, all human languages share similar grammatical features, known as a syntax. Is this merely a coincidence?

It is now commonly assumed that the ability to construct grammatical sentences is relatively independent of other intellectual skills. Children with severe learning disabilities who manage to learn the complexities of speech and grammar even without much general understanding of the world are further evidence of this. (Peter Lloyd discusses language development further in his Open Learning Unit on *Cognitive and Language Development*).

The maturational perspective on human development alerts us to the influence of our genetic make-up on psychological growth and change. Perhaps a fair conclusion is that some biological changes, like puberty, lead to general psychological changes, while others, such as the ability to produce grammatically-correct sentences, appear to develop in a way which is independent of other aspects of development. The 1990s have witnessed a growth in theories claiming that a number of other skills, like thinking, have a biological or maturational basis. Undoubtedly further links between developmental psychology and neurophysiology will be made as advances in technology allow us to study the links between brain structure and function.

Look back at Figure 6 once again. Do the maturational theories imply continuous or stage-like patterns of development?

3. The constructivist perspective

The word 'constructivist' is a bit of a mouthful but it captures an important feature of the third and final perspective on ontogeny: the belief that the crucial ingredient in the development of the individual is neither the genotype nor the environment. Rather it is the interaction between the two that is critical. In Figures 9 and 10 you will see that the environmental and maturation perspectives recognize that genotype and environment have some effect on one another. The constructivist perspective emphasizes the importance of this interaction. Figure 12 presents this graphically.

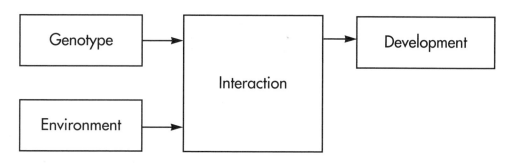

FIGURE 12: *The constructivist perspective.*

If you have been puzzled throughout this section by what the word 'interaction' means, you are not alone. As a twentieth century discipline, developmental psychology is founded upon the question : how, as biological organisms, can we think ? This is a difficult question, and any answer must go beyond the rather circular arguments of the maturation theories that we must have the biological capacity to do these things. The proposed answer is that human beings *construct* an understanding of the world. We are genetically endowed with a means of interpreting events that occur in the environment. It is what we do with these abilities that is important, because psychological processes have to be built upon biological ones using new environmental information as a means of prompting change: genetic and environmental influences interact. So the crucial aspect of development is the gradual way in which humans come to understand the way the world works. Let us look briefly at four constructivist perspectives that try to describe how, as individuals, we come to make sense of the world. Each of these perspectives is discussed at greater length in the companion Units in this series but these brief descriptions will help to show how they all share this common assumption of constructivism.

FIGURE 13: *Sigmund Freud.*

(i) Psychoanalysis : The writings of Sigmund Freud (1856-1939) are usually associated with his views on the causes and treatment of mental disorders. However, he was also a developmental theorist. Not only did he suggest that the problems of adults originate in events and relationships in early childhood, he also claimed that infants and young children develop an emotional style which serves as a basis for personality. For Freud the close physical interaction between infant and mother serves as a blueprint for all later emotional relationships and as a channel for the person's biological drives. How the individual relates to others is largely determined by what Freud calls unconscious processes. These are beliefs and thoughts that cannot be reflected upon by conscious processes partly because they are formed before the infant becomes able to label his or her feelings with words. So what is the difference between psychoanalytic and social learning explanations of development? Psychoanalysis places much greater emphasis on the way in which individuals interpret events. The way in which we construct an understanding of the world is very complex and idiosyncratic according to Freud and his followers.

(ii) Attachment Theory : This theory of emotional development has been very influential over the past quarter century. The psychoanalyst John Bowlby (1907–1991) examined babies aged between 6 months and 2 years. If you know many infants around this age, you will see that they can get very upset when familiar adults, like mum or dad, leave the room, particularly if they are left alone with a stranger. On reunion, they show a variety of behaviours. Most babies display their upset but are calmed easily – they appear to be 'secure', as Bowlby puts it. Others appear to avoid their 'attachment figures' or resist being comforted by them. The companion Unit, *Early Socialization*, by H.R. Schaffer discusses these patterns of behaviour in depth. For our purposes it is important to note that, for Bowlby, children in each of these types of relationship develop a different style of interaction and way of thinking about relationships. This he terms an **inner working model** and for Bowlby it is the basis of all later relationships including how confident the individual will feel in social settings. Attachment theory is constructivist because the child forms his or her own working model based upon a range of experiences. The inner working model becomes more sophisticated as the child's intellectual capabilities develop.

(iii) The Cognitive Perspective : The work of one man, Jean Piaget (1896 –1980), has had the greatest influence on developmental psychology throughout this century. His work has dominated the study of intellectual development : how we come to understand the ways in which the world works starting with only basic biological functions such as reflexes. For

FIIGURE 14: *Jean Piaget.*

Piaget, biological and intellectual growth share common features. The child gradually learns about the world but, every so often, this accumulated learning causes great qualitative changes in the way the individual constructs an understanding of events. Thus Piaget is the quintessential stage-theorist, suggesting that childhood consists of four major intellectual phases, each with its characteristic features. The companion Unit, *Cognitive and Language Development* by Peter Lloyd discusses this theory in detail.

For Piaget, the crucial components in the construction of knowledge are our biologically-driven reactions to the environment. These he calls **schemes** and they are transformed into increasingly complex patterns of action. So a baby initially will suck on its thumb only when the spontaneous movement of the arm leads to the thumb ending up in the mouth. Gradually the infant comes to combine two schemes (put thumb in mouth and suck on thumb) into a more complex and voluntary sequence. The key to this development is the individual's *co-ordination* of such actions.

(iv) The Cultural Perspective : While Piaget stresses the role of the child's construction of knowledge, others have suggested that the essential factor in the genotype–environment interaction is culture. This is an odd word that is used to describe both the arts and what biologists grow their specimens in! However, psychologists use the term to refer to all those social processes which we examined in relation to the theory of Urie Bronfenbrenner (see Figure 2). The key figure in this area is the Russian, Lev Vygotsky (1896 –1934), who wrote an analysis of Piaget's work in the early 1930s, just before his own, very early, death. Vygotsky's writings have grown in influence since they were published in English in the 1960s. He claimed that cultural processes, particularly language, are the key to our understanding of development. The sorts of tools we use, the value systems we espouse and the beliefs and customs we adopt are handed down from one generation to another.

Vygotsky, far more than Piaget, stressed the importance of teaching in the child's development. He felt that the individual acquires a skill by learning it from a more skilled or knowledgeable member of the culture. So children will use words in

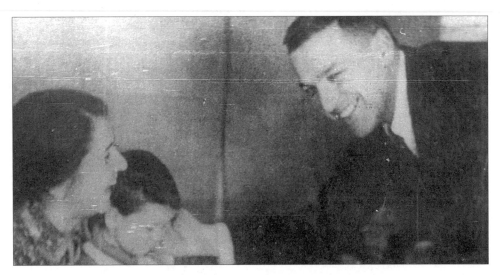

FIGURE 15: *Lev Vigotsky.*

conversation with their parents which they do not fully understand. In such interactions children come to perform skills which they gradually learn to do by themselves. When children learn to ride a bicycle, for example, their parents often run with them, hanging on to the saddle as they pedal along. Gradually the parent's grip becomes less firm until the child is able to cycle alone. Vygotsky's theory suggests that psychological concepts develop in the same way – they are tutored by others until the individual gains mastery over them.

SAQ
8

On the genotype–environment continuum, where would you put the following theories or theoreticians: behaviourism, social learning theory, Piaget, Vygotsky, Bronfenbrenner, maturation theory.

Genotype .... *Environment*

Summary

- ❏ Most developmental psychologists claim that we undergo stage-like changes in which there are discontinuities between how we were and how we are now.

- ❏ Social learning theories emphasize the influence of enviromental pressures on the way in which development unfolds.

- ❏ Maturationists stress the role of the genotype, particularly in areas of development such as language.

- ❏ Most developmentalists emphasize the interaction between the genotype and environment in how we come to construct a continually changing understanding of the world. This process is known as constructivism.

3 Phylogeny: The Evolutionary Development of Different Species

KEY AIMS: By reading this Part you should:

▷ know that non human primates have evolved sophisticated communication systems, particularly about the presence of predators

▷ be familiar with the research on chimpanzee's grasp of symbolic communication and deception

▷ understand the limitation of primates' skills and the advantages of human capabilities.

In Part I of this Unit we saw the influence of evolutionary biology on the origins of developmental psychology. So how similar is the course of human development to that of other species, most notably the great apes? There are two questions here:

• Is the development of particular skills similar across different species?
• How well can individuals from other species perform activities which we deem to be essentially human – language in particular ?

These are complex questions and we shall discuss them in relation to two areas: language and social understanding. Do we, as Darwin thought, share much, if not most, of our abilities with our close relations with whom we have a common ancestor or, as more recent evolutionary theorists have suggested, are we qualitatively different from the great apes in these two essential skills?

Language

Look again at Figure 11. This shows that normal children pick up a large vocabulary very rapidly; but that is only one of the many wonders of the child's

FIGURE 16: Human language emerges so quickly and effortlessly in the second and third years of life.

capability for language. By the age of 3, children can combine words into sentences and make up new combinations. We know this because they often misapply rules. For example 'Mummy buyed some sweets', is a sentence that no adult would utter, but is a common error among preschoolers.

Language enables us to communicate about objects and events in the past and future as well as in the present. As we shall see, most other species communicate about objects which are immediate. Human language can also reflect upon the hypothetical – we could discuss the relative merits of going for a walk on the moon over writing a psychology essay.

Animal communication

How well do animals communicate? Do they use language? Language is symbolic: words stand for actions or objects without necessarily sounding like them. For example, the word 'ball' gives no clue to the spherical nature of the object. Do non-human **primates** use 'words' as symbols? To some extent it seems that they do. One example is the vervet monkey. In the wild, they live in small social groups in shrubland areas and are constantly on the look out for predators such as eagles which attack from the air, and leopards and snakes on the ground. In an intriguing piece of research over many years, Cheney and Seyfarth (1990) have found that, on seeing a predator, a look-out vervet monkey will emit one of three cries. Each has a different effect. The 'eagle alarm' cries will cause the group to scamper into the bushes or search the air for a bird of prey. Two other alarm cries will make them take different evasive actions from the two other types of predator.

The interesting issue here is that the vervet has evolved a communication system which conveys three different signals, all of which are clearly understood. On hearing the leopard cry the group races for the nearest tree – a strategy which would leave no protection against an eagle. So these cries meet the criteria of symbolic communication; they are specific, clearly understood and, most importantly, the sound of each cry does not simply mimic the cry of each predator – the sound *stands for* the predator. Such utterances form the rudiments of language, but do they compare with human communication? There are still qualitative differences between vervet and human 'language'. The two main ones are that humans *combine* sounds into novel communicative patterns (i.e. sentences) and human speech is not as literal as vervet communication.

Teaching 'language' to primates

Perhaps non-human primates *are* capable of these forms of communication but we are insensitive to the subtleties of their 'language'. Over the past 40 years primatologists have attempted to teach higher-order primates, like chimps or orang-utans, to communicate using symbolic systems. Chimps cannot be taught spoken language because their vocal apparatus prevents them from articulating many of the sounds used in human speech, so other systems have been used. In one project David Premack (1971) trained a young chimp, Sarah, to associate tokens of varying shape and colour with objects and actions. Premack found that, like the vervet monkeys, Sarah was able to show that she understood simple relationships such as '*insert apple dish*' in that she would place an apple on a dish after this instruction was given.

FIGURE 17: *A chimp called Nim signing 'dirty' in response to teacher's sign 'house'.*

The case of Sarah shows that chimpanzees can use objects in a comparable way to our employment of words in speech. Yet Sarah might simply have associated strings of tokens without understanding their symbolic (i.e. linguistic) implications. So, many critics suggest that humans are qualitatively different in that their communication system is much more elaborate and spontaneous.

SAQ
9

What are the two main features of human language? Which features do non-human primates fail to demonstrate?

Social understanding

Perhaps higher-order primates lack language skills but still possess other abilities which demonstrate a degree of intelligence which is similar to ours. Over the past 20 years evolutionary theorists have turned some old ideas on their heads. It was long thought that humans came to live in large social groups because we are more intelligent. In 1976, Nicholas Humphrey questioned this assumption. He argued that living in social groups may itself have contributed to an increase in human intelligence. As a result, researchers have intensified their search for comparable skills in other primates. The ability to deceive is one such skill.

Deception

In a series of studies, Judy Dunn (1988) explored just how brothers and sisters get along with each other. To be successful, children sooner or later come to learn that to get their own way they have to trick others into believing things that are not true. If you leave your sweets out on the table they disappear! If you hide them and pretend you don't know where they are then you can return to eat them later when your elder sister is not looking. Children seem capable of this kind of deception around the age of 2, although they may not be fully aware of what they are doing until nearer their fourth birthday.

Do chimpanzees engage in deception and show a similar understanding of how to live in social groups? Careful observation suggests that they have some abilities which match the human preschooler. Whiten and Byrne (1988) give the following example.

Suppose a chimp knows that there are some bananas at one end of the feeding area but that another, more dominant, member of the troop is around. If he moves towards them he will undoubtedly lose his prize. Instead he moves away from the bananas and engages in another activity. When the more dominant chimp moves away, the 'deceiver' makes a dash for the bananas. Such patterns of behaviour are well documented and suggest that chimpanzees have a capacity for 'mind reading', for anticipating and manipulating each other's grasp of events.

Do such capabilities suggest that other species are very like us, and differ only in the degree of skill they can exhibit? While it is tempting to suggest that chimpanzees are remarkably clever, it is always possible that they are less intelligent than they seem. The sorts of deceptive acts described above could be learned by trial and error – going for the banana immediately hasn't worked in the past. So the chimpanzee might learn a covert deceptive ploy without having any understanding of the other's 'mind'.

Experiments with 2-year-olds show that they deceive another person without much hesitation. However they can also, quite unintentionally, deceive someone they are trying to help. A neat example comes from the research of Beate Sodian in Munich (1994). She carried out a game with children in which they had to deceive a 'robber' glove puppet, by hiding a sweet in one container and point to an empty container when the puppet appeared asking where he should look. Two-year-olds could do this without any problem. However, when another 'nice' puppet was introduced who would give the sweet to the child if he was directed to the right container, the child still pointed to the empty container when the nice puppet asked where he should look. In other words children do not fully *understand* what they are doing until a year or so after they first learn to deceive.

Chimpanzees may never know what they are doing. Painstaking research by primatologists such as Daniel Povinelli (Povinelli and Eddy, 1994) strongly suggests that this is the case. He found, for example, that chimpanzees do not seem to grasp the relationship between seeing and knowing. So, if a chimp has two trainers in front of it, one who is looking directly towards her or him, and the other looking directly away, the animal is equally likely to gesture to either for food. There do seem to be qualitative phylogenetic differences between the species.

Conclusion

Both the areas of intellectual competence we have examined, language and social skills, suggest that the differences between humans and their close evolutionary relatives are much greater than they seem on the surface. Language gives us the possibility of reflecting upon events in the past and the future, the possible and the impossible. Social skills like deception may not be very pleasant human attributes but they reflect the apparent fact that we are unique as a species in being able to reflect upon the nature of thinking itself (our own and other people's). This is a major social skill as, coupled with language, it enables us to form much more complex social relationships than members of other species.

Thus the conclusions to the discussions in Part 2 and Part 3 are somewhat similar. Whether you examine ontogeny (the development of the individual) or phylogeny (the evolutionary development over generations) it seems that there are some continuities over time and between species. But the development of an individual, like the capacities of our species in comparison with the great apes (our closest living relatives), shows some discontinuities or qualitative stage-like shifts from one species to another and from one level of individual development to another.

FIGURE 18: *Even in preschool, children become skilled at non-literal communication.*

A health warning about theory in psychology: Right now you might feel that there are so many different views and contrasting perspectives in developmental psychology that it is impossible to tease them apart. This is inevitable: psychology is different from other sciences; it is an intellectual activity reflecting on itself – thinking about thinking. This difference between psychology and other disciplines was pointed out by Heider in 1948. He alerted us to the fact that if psychologists can reflect in this way then so too can everyone. We are all folk psychologists in that we are constantly formulating ideas about our own and others' mental states and the reasons for them. As a result, psychology works in ways different from those of the natural sciences such as physics. In the natural sciences there are much more data for every theory and repeated observations of the same phenomenon. Psychological theory is more reflexive. There is much more debate about the significance of each research finding, and that debate itself is highly informative.

4 Methods in Developmental Psychology

KEY AIMS: By reading this Part you should:
> be able to recall five fundamental issues in the design of developmental research
> understand the strengths and weaknesses of research using observations, experiments and interviews
> have considered the ethical responsibilities of researchers.

In Part 3, I described some examples of research in developmental psychology. Dunn's reflections on sibling relationships stemmed initially from *observations* of brothers and sisters playing. She noted many different types of play, and also conflict between siblings, to give a complete picture of their relationships. Sodian, on the other hand, performed a closely controlled laboratory-based *experiment* in which she changed the deception task slightly to see if children were truly capable of understanding what they were doing.

These two different research methods (observation and experimentation) reflect the diverse influences on developmental psychology which we examined at the start of this Unit. In this section we will examine how we can measure development; which methods should, or may, we use and what are the problems associated with the various types of research design.

SOMETHING TO TRY

Before we start, make a list of the essential ingredients for a study of development. You might find it easier to home in on one of the following areas, as we will examine them later in this Unit: [1] play at different ages or [2] the ability to reflect on what is right and wrong. How can we assess developmental change in these abilities and what problems might occur naturally in any such study?

The central problem: age versus stage differences

Imagine that you want to explore how children come to learn elementary mathematical skills. You test a number of children of different ages on a set of problems ranging from simple addition to complex algebra. You find that there are sharp differences across different age groups – between the ages of 4 and 6 most children's performance on addition improves dramatically and there are similar advances in performance on algebra questions between the ages of 10 and 12. What can you conclude?

You might conclude that some development in the child's understanding of the world during each of these time periods enables him or her really to grasp for the first time the concepts behind the task. In other words, a purely psychological explanation, like a general increase in intellectual skill, is possible.

However, and I suspect you have guessed this, an alternative explanation is possible. It could be that these advances simply reflect changes in the child's daily life and routine. It is highly likely that many children encounter formal addition tasks for the first time when they start formal schooling. It is also possible that they might learn to do simple addition problems without understanding what the calculations actually mean (in terms of a grasp of the underlying properties of number) and without any advances in their intellectual skills taking place. So, we have to distinguish between age differences, which are obvious, and the stages which developmental psychologists identify to explain such age differences.

This example raises the fundamental problem that developmental psychologists face in all their work. This is the relationship between *correlation* and *causation*. Factors like age and mathematical skills may relate to one another, or co-relate – an increase in age is paralleled by an increased mastery of mathematical skills – but that does not mean that age *causes* development. Indeed, by itself, age tells us nothing about the causes of change over the course of life. Developmental psychologists have to search further for the reasons why individuals change as they get older to discover the *nature* of development. A test in which a child adds 2 + 2 helps us to gain some understanding of the child, but we are ultimately interested in his or her grasp of the concept or skill *underlying* the ability to perform such a calculation. The task of the researcher is to reveal causal factors out of a mass of confounding variables, like age in the example above. How can this be done?

SAQ
10

What are the differences between age and stage in development?

Piaget the researcher

In Part 2, I mentioned Piaget's stage theory of development. As well as inspiring many theoretical debates, his distinctive research methods have also been very influential. He studied children for over 50 years and developed procedures known as the *clinical method* (méthod clinique). His approach is given this title because he learned it when he trained briefly in psychoanalysis as a young graduate. The aim of the method is to probe the respondent into giving an accurate account of their experiences. What are the method's characteristic features? Let us consider three of them.

1. **Detailed observation** : Piaget's descriptions of how children tackle particular problems are very meticulous. Starting with the early development of his own children, he was adept at standing back, observing them, recording every move in detail and using his own interpretation of the child's understanding of events. His accounts are highly informative. He describes just how the child (in the following case, his son) approaches and copes with new problems – like the disappearance of an object behind another:

Observation 122:   "At 0:6 [i.e. 6 months of age] I present Laurent with a matchbox, extending my hand laterally to make an obstacle to his prehension [i.e. reach]. Laurent tries to pass over my hand, or to the side, but he does not attempt to displace it" [Piaget, 1953, page 217]

| | "At 0:7 Laurent tries to grasp a new box in front of which I place my hand (at a distance of 10 cm.). He sets the obstacle aside but not intentionally; he simply tries to reach the box by sliding next to my hand and, when he touches it, tries to take no notice of it" [page 217] |
| Observation 126: | "Laurent, at 0:8, plays with a box which I remove from his hands in order to place it under a pillow. Although, four days before, he did not react at all in an analogous situation, this time he at once takes possession of the pillow... Likewise at 0:9, Laurent lifts up a cushion in order to look for a cigar case. When the object is entirely hidden, the child lifts the screen with hesitation, but when one end of the case appears, Laurent removes the cushion with one hand and with the other tries to extricate the object" [page 222] |

2. **Simple, yet revealing tasks** : the example of object permanence : Piaget did not simply observe in minute detail. Intrigued by a range of philosophical questions he devised some simple tasks for *testing* children's knowledge of concepts. The object permanence task is one example. Philosophers have argued for centuries about whether we can be sure that objects (and people) continue to exist when we can no longer perceive them. Piaget wanted to know how babies approach this problem. He therefore hid an enticing-looking toy underneath a cloth or handkerchief. Before eight months of age children appeared to act as if the object had vanished forever; they looked elsewhere for something to do. Piaget did not stop there. He looked at what happens if the object is placed just out of reach on a cushion and within sight. When does the infant realize that if you tug on the cushion the toy comes too? Piaget was so ingenious in designing tasks like these that we are still using them in more formal experiments today.

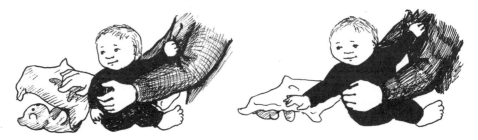

FIGURE 19: *Exploration is an important part of development.*

3. **Exploring depth of understanding** : Earlier we considered just what the success of five-year-olds at simple addition tasks can tell us about their knowledge of mathematical concepts. We concluded that we would need to explore this further. Piaget's genius was to devise ways of making these explorations fruitful to uncover the depths of understanding. He suggests that once children are able to use language we must get them to *justify* their responses when we test them. So, as well as answering the problem 2 + 2 = 4, children must be tested further to show whether they understand the mathematical concepts that underlie such calculations? Do they, for example, also know that 4 - 2 = 2? Children who *fully* understand one of these sums should understand the other. Piaget interviewed

children at length to establish when such knowledge was established. Only when they could justify their answers was Piaget convinced that their understanding was complete.

Piaget also devised clever ways of testing children at an age before they can speak. Let's return to the 8-month-old searching under a cloth for a hidden toy. Does the child fully understand that objects continue to exist even when hidden and no longer in sight? Piaget tested this by hiding the toy under a cloth a few times within full sight of the child, but then hiding it under a second cloth nearby. If the child understands about the permanence of objects he or she should look under the second cloth. However, until twelve months of age, children tend to search under the first cloth, not where they saw the object finally hidden. This suggests that an 8-month-old's understanding of object permanence is far from secure. The companion Unit, *Cognitive and Language Development* by Peter Lloyd examines the theory behind such developments; for our purpose, it serves to demonstrate the methodological innovations made by Piaget.

Why do you think Piaget's method was called the `clinical method'?

What are the three major features of Piaget's approach to studying development?

We will turn now to examine some of the principles upon which most researchers now operate, but it must be stressed that Piaget's methods have had a lasting influence. He showed us the importance of careful observation, simple tasks and how to examine the extent of conceptual understanding. These remain the basic skills of the developmental psychologist.

The basics of research

Before reading on, write a list of procedures which you need to follow in order to conduct a study that assesses development. Which is the most important for our purposes?

There are five fundamental issues in the design of any piece of research: (1) asking an appropriate question; (2) selecting a research design that will most suit the research issue: observation and experiment are the most frequently used techniques; (3) being aware that each research technique has its limitations; (4) realising how research designs help us to address issues of *development*, and (5) considering the ethical implications of the proposed research. Of course, stage (4) is the key question : how do we measure development ?

Asking an appropriate question
This is a key issue in any scientific study, and it is one reason why Part 1 of this Unit examined the diverse theoretical origins of developmental psychology. When we

reflect upon science we think initially of test-tubes and researchers in white coats whose expertise lies in their power of observation. Their theories seem to emerge from these observations. However, this is something of a popular misconception. Philosophers of science (i.e. philosophers who study how science and scientists work) have long pointed out that what scientists choose to observe can be more important than the product, since it is their prior ideas that drive *what* they look at and also *how* they perceive it. Just so in developmental psychology: theory and method are the product of a dynamic interaction.

There are two implications of this. First, methods often reflect the assumptions of a particular era. About 40 years ago, for example, many researchers were keen to understand the effects of various aspects of the child's routine, like toilet training, upon the child. Influenced by psychoanalytic theory they speculated that parental regimes in the child's very early care might have effects on that individual's personality in adulthood. Babies exposed to a routine of being placed on the pot regularly would become highly orderly as a result. They thus devised a range of observational procedures for measuring their impact. Today ideas have changed, and most regard these measures as irrelevant because links between early childhood experiences and adult personality types have been hard to find.

FIGURE 20: *Old and new cultures.*

Secondly, given that our ideas are largely a product of the assumptions of the time, it is always possible to interpret findings in different ways. Researchers have to take great care in considering how the particular methods they use allow them to discriminate between each of these interpretations. The critical questions should always be:

(a) Does this procedure really test the theory concerned? It can do this by providing supportive data or, perhaps more importantly, showing that one's ideas are wrong.

(b) Can the data be interpreted in any other way? If the answer is 'yes', then what further refinements to the procedures can be used to distinguish between alternative explanations? We turn now to examine different types of procedure that can be used.

Types of study

(a) Observation

As we have seen in the case of children's understanding of deception, in Part 3, there are two major types of study in this area: observation and experiment. Observational studies are conducted when the researcher wants to explore what people do in any everyday context. They vary from general descriptions to very detailed analyses. Over the last century there has been a distinct shift from the former to the latter. In the last quarter of the nineteenth century there was a fashion for scientists to write baby biographies – diary accounts of their child's development. As mentioned earlier, Charles Darwin's A *Biographical Sketch of an Infant* (1877) was a description of his son's early life, with some reflections on human evolution.

In the first half of this century, inspired largely by **ethology**, observational studies became more systematic. Not surprisingly this area of research has always had close links with biological theory, particularly the sorts of evolutionary issues described earlier. In the 1950s and 60s the work of ethologists became very detailed. Researchers spent years classifying different types of facial or bodily gesture, so that they could explore the interactions of pairs or groups of individuals. So, for example, when observing one chimp 'deceiving' another researchers like Whiten and Byrne recorded as much of the interaction between that individual and its social group as possible. Close observations determine that a deception really takes place, not random movements of each chimp which result in the individual obtaining by chance what it seems to covet.

In the last 20 years two technological advances have made the science of observation more sophisticated. First, since the 1970s, video recorders have enabled researchers not only to produce film (cheaply) of people interacting, but also to slow down the film and examine interactions repeatedly. They can even look at each of the (usually 25) frames recorded per second to record the details of communication.

One of the earliest of these studies, by Colwyn Trevarthen (1977) in Edinburgh, discovered that when slowed down, the interaction between babies as young as 1 month with their mothers shows a distinctive pattern of what appears to be 'turn-taking'. Babies seem to move their mouths and bodies in a sort of synchronized dance when an adult talks to them. Many researchers have speculated that these 'turns' teach the child the basis of conversation. In adult chat, participants have to talk in sequence and wait their turn, or they are continually interrupting each other and communication is impeded.

FIGURE 21: *Turn-taking.*

The second great advance is the increasing use of computers in research since the 1980s. As computers have become more powerful and more portable, so they have become more useful. Laptop computers are now specially programmed to record particular events. The data are then fed into sophisticated programs in which the minute details of interaction can be explored and statistical analyses conducted.

SAQ 12

To aid your memory, write on the time line when the following techniques were introduced into developmental psychology: the use of computers; baby biographies; ethology; video recorders.

(b) Experiments

If observations are a means of discovering how people act in their daily lives, experimental studies are conducted when the researcher wants to explore why patterns of behaviour occur. The aim is to tease apart different factors that might influence the developmental process under consideration. The experimenter manipulates a limited number of factors (variables) and then measures the result. The companion Unit, *Models and Methods for the Behavioural Sciences*, by Sandy MacRae, describes experiments and observational methods at greater length.

Natural experiments : Sometimes researchers find themselves in the right place at the right time and have the opportunity to conduct what are known as **field** or **natural experiments**. Suppose we found a culture where none of the children went to school, and which chooses to phase in formal education for 5-year-olds. It happens that there are not enough places for all the children, and places are allocated by lottery; only if their name is drawn can they attend. We then have a natural experimental group who attend school and a control group who do not. As long as we can be sure that before schooling begins the two groups are indistinguishable (and we can test for that) on the factors that are important to us, we can then give representative samples of schooled and non-schooled children our simple addition test (see page 28). If schooling is important, then we will find a difference in the performance of the two groups. If another factor is important, then we will expect to find no difference between schooled and non-schooled children of the same age.

The cross-sectional study : Usually researchers are not in the lucky position of being able to do natural experiments, so they have to set up studies in which they manipulate events so that two groups of individuals can be tested and compared. The most basic is the cross-sectional age comparison. Suppose you wanted to investigate if old people become increasingly forgetful, as the popular stereotype suggests. You could then take some adults of different ages across the period defined as 'old age' – three groups at 70, 80 and 90, for example. You could devise a computer-based test to assess their forgetfulness. If memory does decline with age then you would expect worsening performance over the three groups.

There is a flaw in the previous experiment. Can you spot it?

More complex types of experiment involve manipulation of particular groups or procedures. We might give children who do not attend school one of two maths tests. The first could be a formal one in which the sums are written in the way we learned in infant class. The second could be decided in a way more appropriate to how non-schooled children might learn mathematical skills. Over the past 15 years a group of Brazilian researchers has done just this experiment with very poor children who avoid going to school because they have to work as street vendors. These children provide quite a puzzle for developmental psychologists. They use mathematical skills all day, giving correct change to their customers. When given complex real-life tasks, involving the addition of different sets of prices and the amount of change due, they performed well. However, when these same tasks were given as abstract number problems these children performed well below what might be expected from their practical skills (Carraher *et al.* 1985).

The joy of experiments which ask the right questions and are well conducted, is that they can gradually untangle a complex knot of factors contributing to the process of development. The researcher takes experimental data from previous studies and designs a further experiment in order to compare the results. So, we started by thinking about the possible effects of schooling on mathematical skills. I raised the possibility that age differences might arise simply as a result of the fact that as children receive more training at school they also get older. This possibility can be tested if we can find a population where some children attend school and others do not. The studies of Carraher *et al.* show that the picture is more complex – unschooled children can become remarkably proficient at some tasks but only if they are presented in a way that is familiar to them.

SAQ
13

What is the main reason why most developmental psychologists conduct experiments?

 Before reading the next section write down a list of the potential weaknesses in observational and experimental procedures.

Limitations of observations and experiments

So which is the best approach, observation or experiment? Both have limitations. The two procedures are often described as opposites and having different problems. To some extent this is true. Let's look at some of the basic problems which arise from each method.

Potential problems with observational studies :   Observations are made of individuals or groups with no attempt by the investigator to *control* the events – he or she simply reports what happens. The lack of control is seen as the major weakness of this procedure as the ultimate aim of any developmental study is to discover the causes of change. Since observation only records behaviour this does not enable investigators to tease apart *cause and effect*. There is also the suspicion that people may not act naturally when being observed – in other words, the observer influences the behaviour being observed. This is known as the observer or **reactivity** effect. Also, since observers study what occurs in the individual's daily life, there is always the possibility that they record only what those individuals actually do, and ignore what they are capable of doing. Just because we do not ordinarily see chimpanzees deceiving one another does not mean that they cannot engage in all sorts of other 'mindreading' acts. This is sometimes known as the **competence–performance distinction**.

FIGURE22:Observational study: *Siblings working in harmony.*

Potential problems with experiments : Experiments, on the other hand, do try to tease apart cause and effect by manipulating the factors which might contribute to that cause. For this, they are often criticized for attempting to exert too much control on the participants. For example, many experiments take place in settings which are unfamiliar to the participants. Intimidating laboratories in universities might disrupt performance severely particularly where children are involved. It is not always clear that experimenters escape some of the problems found in observational studies. There may also be experimenter effects (like observer effects) and problems of control similar to those discussed in the preceding paragraph.

Addressing these problems : How can we overcome these weaknesses? The first thing we can do is to recognize that research data of any kind are not infallible. They are always open to question and reinterpretation. Normally studies are **replicated** (repeated to see if the same results are obtained) and slightly modified to see if the results hold in a variety of circumstances. It is certainly true that some areas of experimentation have become technically more sophisticated. Later we will examine how we study infant competence as an example of some recent technological advances.

SAQ
14

List at least three criticisms of the observation method and three of the experimental method.

(c) Interviews: a complement to observation and experiment

Psychologists often have to remind themselves that their focus of study is different from those of other scientists. There is an old quip: 'If you want to find out what people are thinking, ask them; they may tell you.'

Interviews are used by developmental psychologists for a number of reasons. In Piaget's clinical method the child should be questioned to see if he or she fully understands the concept of being tested. The experimenter should take pains to challenge the child's knowledge by probing whether he or she can justify an answer in one of the tests that he has devised. If not, then the child is deemed not to have reached the appropriate level of understanding.

Followers of Piaget have used interviews for a number of different purposes. They are employed to examine the development of our grasp of abstract concepts like morality, which we will examine in Part 5. We will look at the ways in which researchers question children's grasp of justice and fairness. Interviews have been widely used to examine the development of our 'theories' about a range of issues, from psychological processes like emotions to our grasp of the world around us. For example, children's understanding of biology develops in interesting ways. Susan Carey (1985) found that pre-schoolers are often adamant that plants are not alive. For them, the definition of being alive is to move about; plants do not fit that description, so they cannot be alive! If basic concepts are to be learned they must come to fit our current knowledge of the world. Change in such knowledge is gradual.

Adults can also be interviewed to discover something about their children or indeed themselves. For a start they can be questioned about the influences on their own and other family members' lives so that the family's 'ecological' circumstances can be understood (see Figure 4). The influences on development are so complex that researchers often need to discover how individuals fit into a web of relationships. In addition, it is useful to know about adults' 'theories' of the influences upon themselves as individuals. For example, we might wish to know which of a range of possible guiding ideas they use as parents. Do they believe in smacking as the best way to deter their children from behaving badly? If so, how often do they use physical punishment on their children and how does this vary according to their children's age? Such topics are best addressed through careful questioning.

From the 1960s onwards interviews became less fashionable than observational and experimental procedures. Social learning theorists questioned whether interviews produced truly objective (i.e. factual) data. However, since the 1980s they have become more frequently used since it has been realized that no single method provides all the answers in developmental psychology. Interviews provide essential evidence about the range and complexity of beliefs that influence our actions.

SAQ
15

List at least two issues which can be addressed using interviews.

SOMETHING TO TRY

Interviews are relatively easy to carry out although in fact they are a difficult means of gleaning valid data. Try interviewing either a pre-school child of 4 or 5 or their parent. Ask the child questions about whether certain objects are alive: cats, teddy bears, flowers, statues and anything else that you feel may be interesting. Remember to follow up your questions with probes to test the child's understanding.

Alternatively, ask a parent about their attitudes towards smacking children : is it an important means of showing children what is right or wrong? How old should children be before parents use it? How often should children be smacked? What do the answers you get to questions like these tell you about the adult's `theory' of discipline?

Is there a 'developmental method'?

Most of the methods discussed so far apply in all areas of psychology not only developmental psychology. Observation has been used in social psychology and experiments are a central feature of cognitive psychology. Yet there are some aspects of these procedures which are essentially developmental. These all stem from the central feature of developmental psychology: the study of change in individuals. I have already mentioned the procedure which is used predominantly in developmental research: the **cross-sectional** study in which two or more age groups are compared at any one point in time. Yet, strangely, this procedure is not exactly a developmental one. Can you think why? If we simply compared the butterfly in Figure 6 with other pupae or caterpillars we would not be assessing the critical features of their development – the **metamorphosis** from one form to another. The trouble with cross-sectional studies is that they study *differences between age groups*, not the *mechanism of change.*

Cross-sectional comparisons have distinct advantages. The obvious one is that they are highly efficient of time and money. I raised the example of forgetting. If we wish to compare old people's ability to remember things, a project following the same individuals at ages 70, 80 and 90 would be impracticable. Not only would it take years to complete the study but, unfortunately, many of the participants would have died before the end of the period (this is a clue to the answer to the question about the problem with the experiment described on page 32). So most developmental psychologists cut corners and compare age groups.

(d) The longitudinal study

The truly developmental research design is the *longitudinal study.* Here the same individuals are investigated over the course of development (or part of it). The period of time may be short, for example a few weeks in a baby's life, or over a significant transition such as the first few days at school.

At the other extreme there are what are often known as **cohort studies**. These take large numbers of children born in the same week or month and follow them at regular intervals throughout their lives. There have been three such major studies conducted in Britain since the Second World War with data collected on thousands of participants.

National child development study: an example of a cohort study

Within one week in March 1958 around sixteen thousand children were born in the United Kingdom. The National Child Development study was set up to investigate the health and education patterns of these children. Around 13,000 were studied over the course of their childhoods. This survey matches two other cohorts born in one week in March 1946 or April 1970. Like other surveys, data collected over such a long period of time enables us to compare the development of children in different time periods and at many stages of development. So we can see whether the cohort born immediately after the Second World War did as well at school as those born in the more prosperous 1970s.

The advantage of longitudinal designs is that they enable us to examine the many possible contributors to developments and measure the importance of each to the individuals concerned. Let's take an example: the impact of divorce on children. Cross-sectional studies suggested that the separation between parents was associated with their children having more problems at school, with relationships and in feelings of depression. (In fact these problems are not as great as many political commentators have suggested, but that is another matter.) But are these the result of the parents' separation? Longitudinal analyses of large cohorts in Britain and the United States have examined whether the act of separation is the cause or whether other factors are involved. In one investigation, researchers took all those children in one age group (eg 7–11) whose parents had separated. They were interested to see if these children were different from the others in the sample *before* the separation took place, and in fact found that this was the case. So they were able to establish that divorce is not the cause of children's problems – these go further back than the act of parental separation (Cherlin *et al.* 1991).

Longitudinal research enables us to compare the influence of a range of factors over time but it has obvious disadvantages. Not only is it very costly and time consuming to follow up individuals but people have a habit of moving (and dying) and are often lost to the researcher before a study can be completed. There is also the issue of observer effects. Suppose I test your knowledge of developmental psychology now and tell you that I will come back and re-test you in a few weeks' time. You might work hard at your studies in that period to impress me at the second test. Or, you might be annoyed at further interference from a researcher and decide to mess up the second test. Like psychologists themselves, their 'subjects' can be influenced by the research process and longitudinal research studies have to consider these effects. These problems are hard to overcome but can usually be minimized. So if participants are forewarned about the need to collect data on a second occasion and are told why this is necessary they are usually co-operative.

(e) Intervention study

A further research technique should be mentioned. This is the *intervention study*. It is used essentially to examine the competence/performance distinction mentioned earlier. Suppose we want to see if formal maths teaching is more important than the individual's age or general developmental stage. We might train 3-year-olds in simple addition and see if such training enables them to perform as well as schooled 6-year-olds. The research would therefore have a teaching phase followed by a test (the experiment). The intervention would help to show if the ability to perform simple maths calculations is learned in isolation from all other skills picked up between the ages of 3 and 6. The advantage of such a study is that it allows researchers some control over events. So they might set up two different teaching strategies to compare their effects. These experiments often produce interesting results; however, they also have their problems. As in longitudinal studies, interventions by experimenters may give rise to unexpected findings or changes which would not happen in normal development. We will look at an example of the complexities of intervention when we examine play and learning in Part 5.

SAQ 16

Name three of the main methods used in developmental psychology?
What are their strengths and weaknesses?

The various methods that I have described here should not be seen as opposing techniques. Each produces different results and they are complementary to one another. You might start an investigation with a cross-sectional study to see when a particular ability emerges, or differs, between particular age groups. Then you could follow-up a group of individuals in a short-term longitudinal investigation over the transitional age pinpointed in your cross-sectional study. Finally you could manipulate some of the potentially important contributing factors in an intervention study to tease out which is the crucial one.

Ethical issues

No consideration of research methods in developmental psychology would be complete without some discussion of the ethical factors and dilemmas which may arise. Children are the prime focus of much of the research: we want to discover when and how abilities emerge. It would be easy to cajole children into participating in research. Suppose that you approach students in a college bar and ask if they would participate in an experiment involving simple arithmetic. Are you infringing their rights? Most ethical guidelines would suggest that as long as they are not coerced (and are free to say 'no') such a way of approaching participants is acceptable as long as they are fully aware of what the experiment involves and are free to leave it at any time. What if you approach a 6-year-old in the school classroom. Does that child understand what you are asking? Is he or she aware of their right to say that they don't want to participate? Children are much more at the mercy of the experimenter than are adults, and special attention should be paid to their rights and their vulnerabilities.

The British Psychological Society has produced clear and detailed guidelines about what it regards as acceptable research practice. If you carry out any study, particularly if it involves children, you should consult these (and you should read the companion Unit *Ethics in Psychological Research and Practice*, by Alison Wadeley). As a rule of thumb the following questions should be addressed before any study is carried out.

- Have you informed the participant fully about the nature of your study?

- Have you sought permission for the study? In order to work in institutions you need permission from the person in charge (e.g. the head teacher).

- Have you obtained the participant's consent? It is customary now for participants (or those in charge of them) to sign special consent forms which also describe what the study is about.

- Have you told the participant that they are free to stop their participation at any time if they want to?

- Have you kept all the results safe and confidential?

- If you have had to conceal part of the aims of the research from participants have you sought counsel from your tutors or colleagues about whether such an action is necessary or desirable? After the experiment have you explained why you deceived them and allowed them to withdraw their 'data' if they wish?

Summary

Having read this Part you should be aware of some of the key principles of research within developmental psychology.

- ☐ Studying change is not easy. To begin with we have to account for *why* development takes place.

- ☐ Pointing out age differences does not tell us a developmental story.

- ☐ It was Piaget who was master of designing methods for exploring the complexity of development. Simple tasks, careful observation and detailed explanations of the individual's understanding are needed.

- ☐ Modern developmental research uses experiments and observations in the main, but interviews can also be employed.

- ☐ The most fundamental issue concerns the framing of the research question. This guides the way in which a study is both conducted and interpreted.

- ☐ We have to select the type of study which most suits this research question.

- ☐ We must be aware that no single research technique provides all the answers – we must work within the limits of each.

- ☐ We must be aware of what methods are particularly relevant to developmental psychology. Longitudinal designs and intervention studies are often the most appropriate.

- ☐ Finally, we must be mindful of the ethical issues involved in research, particularly where children are involved.

5 Three Areas of Research : Infant Perception, Play and Moral Development

In this Part we will examine three areas of research to illustrate some of the points that have been made in the previous discussions of theory and method.

The first area, infant perceptual skills, reveals some of the ingenuity that researchers have brought to their studies. The second looks at play, since research on this topic involves all the traditions described in Figure 2 (philosophy, evolutionary biology, social policy and culture) and all the methods described in the previous section. Finally, we will consider moral development – how children acquire an understanding of what is considered to be appropriate moral conduct. This allows us to explore how developmentalists make theories about different stages of development.

Technology and studies of infant perception

(?) *How skilled are newborn babies at focusing on objects around them? How do you think you could test their abilities?*

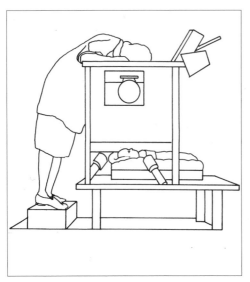

Earlier I mentioned the introduction of video recorders and computers into research in the 1970s. These are only two of many changes which have revolutionized research. One area of study in particular, the baby's ability to discriminate between different objects, illustrates some of these.

FIGURE 23: *Fantz's looking chamber.*

How early in life do infants learn to recognize small differences in colour, texture and shape? Do babies automatically realize that an object is the same if it is rotated slightly? As recently as the 1950s many researchers observed the movements of infants' eyes and limbs to be poorly co-ordinated and interpreted that as a sign of their perceptual and intellectual incompetence. However, partly as a result of the writings of Piaget, technological innovations were introduced into research particularly after the Second World War. A landmark was the development of the '*looking chamber*' by the American psychologist, Robert Fantz. This is essentially an apparatus that a baby is placed inside lying on his or her back. In front of the child is a white surface on to which can be placed 2D and 3D shapes. Initially Fantz and his colleagues used a procedure to examine infants' visual competence known as **spontaneous visual preference**. Here the infant is presented with two shapes side-by-side – a cross and a circle for example – on the screen in front of it. Between the shapes is a small hole through which an experimenter can watch the infant's 'preference' for one pattern over the other. From birth infants systematically look longer at patterns than at plain coloured cards. Their 'favourites' are a schematic representation of a face and a sequence of concentric circles, similar to a dart board.

The spontaneous visual preference technique reveals that newborn babies can discriminate between different shapes but it does not allow experimenters to make very close measurements in infants' skills. Other procedures have been developed to look more closely at their responses to visual stimuli. A major one is known as the **habituation/dishabituation** (or habituation/novelty) procedure. If infants are presented with a new stimulus they tend to look at it more often and for longer than at a familiar object. Attention slowly wanes and habituation sets in. The use of this method comes about when a new stimulus is introduced to replace the old one. If the baby can discriminate between the two objects or pictures then he or she will look more at the new one. This is known as dishabituation. It is perhaps a relief from boredom! The dual processes are shown in Figure 24.

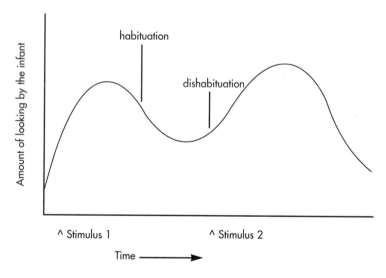

FIGURE 24: *Habituation and dishabituation in infants looking at objects.*

The pattern of looking described in Figure 24 is useful as it shows what would be expected if infants can indeed discriminate between different stimuli. Suppose a maltese cross, spinning slowly in an anticlockwise direction, is placed in front of the child. After initial interest in it for around two minutes, he or she habituates to it.

What happens if the rotation of the cross is reversed, so that it now turns in a clockwise direction, as shown in Figure 25? Do babies dishabituate to it? If they do, this would suggest that they regarded it as a novel object. not as the one they had seen before. Alan Slater *et al.* (1985) found that 3-day-old children did not dishabituate – they seemed to appreciate that the cross was the same despite its change in rotation.

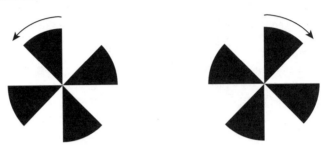

FIGURE 25: *The rotating cross used in Slater et al's experiment.*

Other uses of the habituation/dishabituation technique discern infants' skills when dishabituation occurs. For instance, we have considered the development of simple mathematical abilities in examples throughout this Unit. When do children acquire an understanding of number? Antell and Keating (1983) used the procedure to discover whether 2-day-olds can distinguish different quantities from one another. They presented to the children arrays consisting of different numbers of large black dots. The infants dishabituated when four dots in a row replaced two dots but not if they replaced six dots, as shown in Figure 26. The top two rows show two of the pairs of trials in which the newborn babies successfully dishabituated (i.e. they showed renewed interest in the right-hand array when it replaced the left-hand one). However, in the bottom two rows when more dots were used there was no renewal of looking when the right-hand array replaced the left one. Thus it seems as if very young babies can 'count' up to four (!), or at least they are able to distinguish the number of items presented, presumably because of the complexity of the overall pattern.

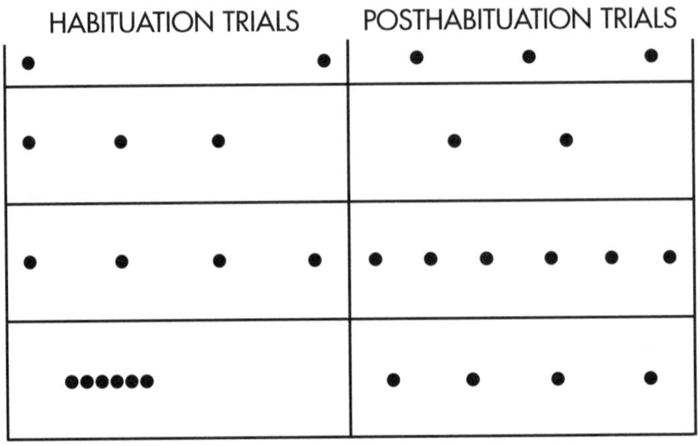

HABITUATION TRIALS	POSTHABITUATION TRIALS
• •	• • •
• • •	• •
• • • •	• • • • • •
••••••	• • • •

FIGURE 26: *Four sets of stimuli used by Antell and Keating (1983). Note that in each procedure the baby habituates to the array on the left, which is then replaced by the one on the right.*

Why do you think that Antell and Keating used four sets of procedures? Would two have been enough?

In this brief description of infant perception I have singled out two research procedures because they are ingenious yet simple. In many respects research has now moved on, with techniques for measuring heart rate and brain activity being used in addition to assess whether the infant takes an interest in various stimuli. Methods are now used to examine the movements of the eye by filming the child's direction of gaze. We thus know that babies tend to scan the edges of objects and/or small parts where the contrast between dark and light is greatest. It is also possible to film, through the front of the eye into the retina, the surface of nerve cells which transmit what we see to the brain. These methods give us extraordinary insight into the ways in which babies perceive the world. Initially they see objects in a blurred way, like an out-of-focus camera, because the structure of the eye and the strength of its muscles do not allow the image to be focused properly. Gradually, over the first year, children come to focus and scan objects more efficiently.

SAQ
17

How have researchers been able to discover the skills of newborn infants?

Play: issues of phylogeny and ontogeny

Discussion about the relevance of play to human development is not new, but the issue rose to prominence this century largely due to the reflections of evolutionary biologists inspired by Darwin. They noted that, like children, animals spend much of their time doing things that appear to have no direct relevance to survival. Chimpanzees engage in rough and tumble chasing games and mock fighting – children, too, 'monkey around'. In this analysis we shall consider

(a) the evolutionary significance of play

(b) how to define the term, and

(c) the role of play in development.

What are the characteristics of play? What do the following have in common? A dog chasing a ball; lambs frisking in the field; a child sailing a toy boat? Jot down your ideas.

Phylogeny and development

In the late nineteenth century biologists speculated about why immature animals and children engage in activities which are not directed towards anything useful. Authors like Herbert Spencer (*The Principles of Psychology*, 1898) declared that play is little more than an expression of surplus energy and has no bearing upon the process of development. This view was directly criticized by the two books of Karl Groos (*The Play of Animals*, 1899, and *The Play of Man*, 1901) which stressed the potential of play in preparing the young for adulthood. Groos's theories tapped into a tradition within educational theory which stressed the importance of exploration in development, most notably the German Friedrich Froebel, who opened the first kindergarten school in 1836 and the Italian Maria Montessori, who developed her own schools for 3-to 6-year-olds from 1907. Later theories have tended to suggest that play helps the child to *practise* skills in a context which, being divorced from reality, does not expose him or her to real danger. So in play-fighting the young learn about self-protection without the risk of being hurt. To what extent does this notion of play-as-practice help us to understand the concept?

Unfortunately this idea is open to much interpretation but few testable hypotheses. Most authorities have tended to mix some of Spencer's ideas with those of Groos. Psychologists such as Sigmund Freud and Melanie Klein (a prominent twentieth century British psychoanalyst) have suggested that children express their unconscious fears and fantasies in play, allowing them to address deep inner conflicts. Piaget argued that play allowed the child to practise skills learned during everyday activities. He was adamant as a result that they do not use play to learn new skills. These views contrast with the claims of Jerome Bruner in the 1970s, who argued that the very fact that children consider ideas and projects together helped in the process of learning. Like Groos, Bruner saw play as a process of mastering new skills within a safe context.

FIGURE 27: *Children playing in a sand tray.*

Does play develop in a stage-like way?

So some theories state that play merely allows the practice of previously learned skills, while others claim that it allows new skills to be acquired. Which set of theories is correct? To my mind it has been impossible to deliberate between the two positions with a neat set of research findings. Let's look at the belief that play reflects cognitive development.

In 1932, the American, Mildred Parten, published a study in which she described five levels of social play (i.e. play involving pairs or groups) in pre-school children aged between 2 and 5:

1. **Solitary:** The child plays alone with little or no interactions with those around him or her.

2. **Onlooker:** The child merely watches others without participating.

3. **Parallel:** Children appear to participate with one another in that they play with the same apparatus (e.g. the sand tray). However, in reality they do not interact except to copy one another's activities.

4. **Associative:** Children may talk about their parallel activities but do not undertake a joint project in play.

5. **Collaborative:** The participants jointly agree upon the aims of the activity and divide up tasks.

FIGURE 28: *The child as onlooker.*   FIGURE 29: *Solitary play.*

Parten suggested that as children become more intellectually capable they progress from the first three levels of play up to the last two. This implies that the complexity of play increases with development in a stage-like way. It has been suggested that perhaps humans progress through stages of development characteristic of the skills of other species before engaging in higher-level activities like co-operation. Research using cross-sectional studies suggests that the sequence suggested by Parten is correct.

However, some longitudinal studies show that the position is more complicated. For example, Harper and Huie (1985) looked at a class of preschoolers over the course of a nursery school year and found that, within that year, solitary activity declined and cooperative play increased. It seems that the transition from one extreme to the other depends as much upon the familiarity of playmates as upon intellectual capacity. Harper and Huie's study serves to show both the importance of longitudinal studies and the problems with fixed 'stage' theories.

Describe the two main theories of play. Can you think of ways of testing their relative merits?

A POSSIBLE PROJECT

If you have access to a pre-school group or nursery school spend an hour or so watching the children going about their daily activities. You will need to get permission from the person in charge. Record the children's activities and try to categorize the types of play they engage in. The following list may serve as a guide.

Defining play

Look back at your notes on the characteristics of play which you made at the start of this discussion. You might like to compare what you wrote with what psychologists have found. First though, here is a list of the types of play that are discussed.

1. **Rough and tumble:** This varies from tickling with babies, through chasing games with young children and play-fighting in children as old as teenagers.

2. **Symbolic play:** This involves substituting one object for another. The 18-month-old who pretends to drink from a doll's cup is engaging in pretend or symbolic play. More complex forms include fantasy games.

3. **Ritual play:** These are repetitive and rhythmic games in which children engage in gestures or words with exaggerated expression. These might be simple exchanges, as in 'peek-a-boo' games with babies, or more complex language play.

4. **Games with rules:** These become more evident as the child grows older. They are seen clearly in activities such as football or hopscotch in the school playground, and were also seen in role-playing (e.g. doctors and nurses) in the playgroup.

FIGURE 30: *Games with rules.*

SAQ
19

Write the following games in a column on the left-hand-side of a piece of paper. Categorize each one using one (or perhaps two) of the types of play described in points 1 to 4 above.

- chess
- cops and robbers
- 'tig' or 'tag' (where a child is 'on' and has to catch one of the others)
- making up rhymes
- netball
- 'cooking' in the Wendy house
- grandmother's footsteps
- Simon says
- answering an SAQ.

This list gives you an idea of how different types of play can be classified. How can we tell whether an act is playful or not? Sometimes, for example, it is very hard to tell the difference between play-fighting and actual fighting. Where, and why do we draw such lines? Of the many attempts to define play perhaps the clearest and most widely-used system is that of Krasnor and Pepler (1980). They argue that for an act to be playful it must contain all of the following characteristics. It must :

(a) show *positive affect* : put simply, it must be enjoyable;

(b) be *non-literal* : it cannot serve any literal purpose – so pouring tea is not playful unless, for example, you pour 'pretend' tea;

(c) include *flexibility* : it cannot simply be an act repeated endlessly – the players must introduce new ideas and activities;

(d) include *intrinsic motivation* : it must not be impressed on the player, but be done voluntarily and for its own sake.

How watertight is this definition? Does it match your own? How can we measure its use in research and theory? We will reflect on its theoretical relevance at the end of this section; for now we will consider whether we can agree upon what these criteria identify. One way is to see whether independent observers agree about whether an action (classed as playful) fulfils each of the four characteristics. Smith and Vollstedt (1985) videoed children in a nursery school. Each clip was rated by 70 adults according to (a) whether or not it showed the child playing and, if so, (b) which of the four defining characteristics it fitted.

There was high agreement over what was playful and what was not. Playful acts were also seen to be *non-literal*, *flexible* and to contain *positive affect* (enjoyment). But intrinsic motivation did not stand up to the test – the adult judges did not necessarily rate playful acts as voluntary. It is relatively easy to judge what people are doing and their reactions to it. However, it is hard to judge their motives for their actions. We thus have to rely upon what we see. As Smith and Cowie (1991:171) put it : 'The main criteria so far identified for play in young children are enjoyment, flexibility and pretence'. We know what play is, but do we understand its role in development?

SAQ
20

What are the four criteria for play defined by Krasnor and Pepler? How have psychologists assessed whether these criteria really define play?

Play and learning

One way of demonstrating the role of play in development is to examine its influence on specific abilities. Authors such as Jerome Bruner have claimed that play allows the child to combine and refine a range of skills and causes learning. In the 1970s a series of intervention studies appeared to demonstrate such learning. We will examine this tradition, as it also shows the complexities of this type of research.

In 1977, Kathy Sylva compared the effectiveness of play versus instruction in pre-schoolers. She set up a task in which a child is seated at a table; out of reach is a box which contains a reward (a sweet or crayon is used) which the child is told he or she can keep if they get it. The child is supplied with two sticks and a clamp. Neither stick is long enough on its own to reach the box – they have to be clamped together. Sylva divided the children into two groups. In the *experimental condition* they were allowed to play with the sticks and clamp before they were told to try to get the reward. The *control group* did not play, but instead were told (but not shown) how to solve the task by clamping the sticks together.

FIGURE 31: *Play and learning.*

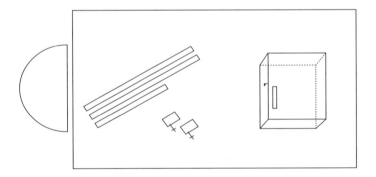

FIGURE 32: *The sticks, clamps and box used in Sylva's play and learning experiment.*

(?) *Which group, the experimental or the control group, do you expect to succeed best?*

You might expect the control group to solve the task more easily, since they were told explicitly how to do it; all the experimental group did was to play with the materials first. In fact, playing led to greater success in the task, as these children needed fewer additional hints on how to obtain the reward. Sylva's research seemed to show that simply *exploring* materials teaches children more effectively than explicit instruction. These results and others like them have been **replicated** and the results confirmed the original findings.

Sylva's experiment was well conducted. It compared two groups and had a clear outcome measure of success – retrieving the reward. The replications add to our confidence that the results are reliable. However, this does not mean that the data should not be re-examined. Indeed, the aim of research should be to explore procedures from every vantage point.

In 1984, Peter Smith and Tony Simon published a series of experiments which appear to undermine Sylva's results. They conjectured that the difference between the experimental and control groups in this task may not be to do with the fact that one played with the materials beforehand while the other did not. Perhaps the experimenter unwittingly influenced the results of such experiments. To control for this possibility Simon and Smith's experiments involved two experimenters – one to allocate the children into the two groups and supervise the play or instruction, the other to measure children's performance on the retrieval task but being unaware of which children were in each group. This type of procedure is known as a **blind trial** because neither experimenter is allowed access to the other's part in the procedure. Simon and Smith's results failed to show the advantages of playing with the materials first, and they concluded that the original positive results may be the result of 'experimenter effects'. So, to date, we have no conclusive evidence that play influences learning.

Can you think of an alternative reason why Simon and Smith's experiments produced non-significant results?

This brief analysis has shown that the topic of play is far more complicated than the lay person might think. We all know roughly what play is and researchers can come to some agreement on a definition. We saw that three characteristics of play can be agreed upon. However, beyond this there are problems in discerning the role of play in development.

Play and cultural values

The discussion on play and learning shows how difficult it is to design experiments. It also suggests how difficult it is to relate specific abilities (like retrieving something out of reach in Sylva's experiment) to the sorts of skill practised during play. Recent theoretical analysis suggests that one of the major problems in understanding play stems from the rather limited definition of the concept which has been drawn from evolutionary biology. We have tended to consider play in terms of comparisons between humans and other species. Even Sylva's experiment was based on an earlier observation of chimpanzees using a stick to retrieve a banana.

A theoretical analysis by Sutton-Smith and Kelly-Byrne (1984) has been influential on our current understanding of play. They suggest that we have relied too heavily upon biology as a source of our theories and not enough on the other influences, such as those outlined right at the start of this Unit in Figure 1. Social policy is an important issue.

The term 'play' was first used in academic discussion of human development at the end of the nineteenth century. This occurred partly because industrial cultures faced serious juvenile problems. Play was seen as a therapy for children who would otherwise be on the streets and also as a means of controlling wayward youths. Even today, social programmes which emphasize play (such as nursery schools for deprived children or the famous Head Start programme in the USA) make the assumption that play is a useful means of learning and of controlling potentially difficult children. Yet, as we have seen, the relationship between play and learning is difficult to identify. Sutton-Smith and Kelly-Byrne have made us reflect upon our culture's general attitudes towards play. They argue strongly that powerful vested interest groups, like the toy industry, rely upon the concept of play being an important part of our heritage. Developmental psychologists might perpetuate an interest in the concept not because they have insightful ways of theorizing about it but because there are cultural pressures on us to maintain an interest. As I have stated so often before in this Unit, developmental psychology reflects cultural values just as much as it provides new information about the way we think, feel and act.

SAQ
21

What are the main points in Sutton-Smith and Kelly-Byrne's criticism of the concept of play? (Do you agree with them?)

Are there stages in moral development?

As Figure 1 shows, developmental psychology has been influenced by pressing social and philosophical debates. Researchers have long been concerned with why some individuals become upstanding members of the community, while others do not. The 1990s have witnessed an increase in reported teenage delinquency, particularly 'joy-riding'. As discussion on these issues is widespread it seems hard to conduct research which is balanced in terms of making appropriate interpretations of the available data. There are so many viewpoints expressed in the media about the causes of 'immorality' in the young that the topic of moral development is a theoretical minefield.

Developmental psychologists have devised many ways of exploring young children's moral development. Their studies divide broadly into the two types which reflect the two major procedures described earlier – observation and experiment. Researchers using observational techniques tend to examine what is termed **prosocial behaviour** – actions which are supportive of others, particularly when someone obviously needs help. The major issue involves the age at which children demonstrate various types of action like comforting a sibling who has fallen over or helping a parent with domestic

FIGURE 33: *Altruism is a key feature of human development.*

chores. Research shows clearly that these are seen in children before their second birthday. The problem with such findings is that it is hard to distinguish acts which are simply copied from those which the individual carries out as a result of moral duty.

Moral reasoning

The experimental tradition, on which we shall concentrate here, has examined the child's understanding of the rules of moral conduct, often referred to as *moral reasoning*. Here, children are given hypothetical problems and they have to explain why someone acted in a particular way or, alternatively, what they should do in a particular situation. Careful questioning can assess the complexity of their thinking on these matters.

As in many other areas of research, studies of moral reasoning have been greatly influenced by the thinking and experiments of Piaget. In 1932 he published a series of studies in which he set children moral dilemmas to solve. Two typical examples are as follows:

There are two children. Tom is asked to do a job for his mother. On his way into the kitchen he breaks a trayful of cups and saucers by accident.

Camilla is doing something she knows she should not, like reaching for some food in the kitchen. While doing so she knocks over a cup and saucer.

Children are told a story about these two characters and are asked which child is the naughtier. Those aged 5 to 10 usually say that Tom is the naughtier as he broke more cups. Only from the age of 11 do children say that Camilla is more naughty as she was doing what she was not supposed to be doing.

What if Andrea has been told never to climb a tree (because it is dangerous) but she sees her friend's kitten hanging precariously from one of its top branches? Should she break her promise just this once to rescue the kitten?

FIGURE 34: *Moral developments.*

Before the age of 7 children appear to say no, since a rule is treated as inviolate. Over the age of 7 children adopt a relativist stance, saying that in this special circumstance it is acceptable to break the rule.

External and internal morality

For Piaget there are two major stages in the development of a moral code. Up to the age of 11 children believe in **external morality**. Rules are seen as inflexible and the moral implications of an action are connected to their consequences rather than the reasons behind them. So during this stage children cannot say what a moral rule is. From the age of 11 children develop an **internal**, or **autonomous morality**. They no longer believe that rules are sacrosanct, and base their assessment of moral dilemmas according to the intentions of the actor. In other words, children shift from a code of absolute moral values to one of relative values. They do this as a result of their increasing cognitive abilities.

Lawrence Kohlberg's three levels of moral development

The dominant theoretician in the field of moral development over the past 40 years is Lawrence Kohlberg. He took Piaget's ideas about the two stages of moral development (external and internal) and modified and extended them to include development in adolescence and adulthood. He did this using experiments in which participants had to give their solution to more complicated moral dilemmas, such as the following:

> In Europe, a woman was near death from a special kind of cancer. There was one drug that the doctor thought might save her. It was a form of radium that a druggist in the same town had recently discovered. The drug was expensive to make, but the druggist was charging 10 times what the drug cost him to make. He paid $200 for the radium and charged $2,000 for a small dose of the drug. The sick woman's husband, Heinz, went to everyone he knew to borrow the money, but he could only get together about $1,000 — half of what it cost. He told the druggist that his wife was dying, and asked him to sell it cheaper or let him pay later. But the druggist said 'No, I discovered the drug and I'm going to make money from it.' So Heinz got desperate and broke into the man's store to steal the drug for his wife.

Kohlberg asked participants whether Heinz was right to steal the drug. He found that they answered this question in ways which changed systematically with age. Like Piaget he believed that this was a reflection of their abilities to think in increasingly complex ways, and such developments occur in stages. Kohlberg's model of development contains three *levels*, each consisting of two *stages*. Children are thought to progress from one stage to the next in a fixed, logical sequence.

Level 1: pre-conventional moral reasoning. The first level is what Kohlberg terms pre-conventional moral reasoning. As in Piaget's 'external' stage, children at this level are preoccupied with getting rewards and avoiding punishment:

Stage 1 is concerned with punishment and obedience. For Kohlberg such children follow **heteronomous** moral rules, in other words, rules which are imposed by others. They base moral judgments purely in terms of avoiding being punished or doing what you are supposed to do. So, in response to the above dilemma, some say that Heinz should not steal the drug as he may be put in prison; others that he should take the drug as it is only worth $200.

Stage 2 children begin to weigh up the pros and cons of the dilemma : the central issue concerns the individual's self-interest in the face of what might occur if a rule is transgressed. They set the possibility of prison against Heinz's aim to help his wife. This stage is known as an **'instrumental-exchange'** approach to moral rules. Those in favour of the theft may say he might go to prison but he would still have his wife. Those against might suggest that he should not steal the drug as the druggist's job is to make money. So, while children may come to see both points of view by the end of the preconventional 'period', they do not weigh them fully against one another. Kohlberg argued that most children cease to reason in this way at around age 9, but some wayward teenagers and adult criminals may never develop beyond this way of looking at moral rules.

Level 2: conventional moral reasoning. At the next level children are less concerned with the immediate (selfish) needs of the individual. They reflect more upon what societal rules are appropriate and justifiable. The Heinz dilemma is a balance between being 'dutiful' to those you love and maintaining a fairly rigid set of moral conventions and laws.

In *Stage* 3 (which has no quick and easy title) being good is assessed by acting according to how you are expected to act. Heinz should steal the drug because he loves his wife and family commitments override any other rules. Alternatively, if they say he should not take it they condemn the druggist as heartless.

In *Stage* 4, a concern for the good of the family extends into a concern for society. This is often known as the **law-and-order** stage as respondents couch their judgments in terms of his marriage contract 'to cherish your wife' obliging him to override another law 'not to steal'. If respondents come out against the theft they point out Heinz's view but state that the law of the land is more important. According to Kohlberg, most adults adhere to a system of conventional morality.

Level 3: post-conventional moral reasoning. This third level is acquired only by about one-fifth of adults and usually not until after the age of 20. Here each person is credited with his or her own principles of justice – not simply those that are handed down by convention. At this level all judgments are seen in relativist terms, respecting the individual's rights and duties within a range of culturally diverse viewpoints.

In *Stage* 5 a **social contract orientation** is adopted. Here rules are regarded as arbitrary but respected because they are generally for the common good. So, if life is taken to be more important than property, not only is it 'right' to steal the drug for your spouse, but there are also grounds to do the same thing for your friend or even a complete stranger.

In *Stage* 6, the individual follows a code of **universal ethical principles** based upon concepts like equality, justice and respect for all human rights. These go beyond any decision based on a society's laws or codes and any interests of self or family. The obvious example of someone who lives by such a code is Mother Teresa of Calcutta who works selflessly for her beliefs.

SOMETHING TO TRY

Give the Heinz dilemma to two or three friends. At what stage of development would you classify their responses? Is it easy to fit their responses to such a classification?

I have gone into the details of Kohlberg's model to give you a feel for the complexity of stage theories and also the way in which subtle qualitative shifts distinguish one stage from the next. A small intellectual transition is marked by regarding the world in radically different ways. How can we test Kohlberg's theory? He did so in the two ways with which you are now very familiar. Kohlberg, with others, has done many cross-sectional studies, finding that, by and large, the older the individual the higher his or her stage of moral development. He also carried out a 20-year longitudinal study of a group of boys in Chicago, interviewing them every four years. Kohlberg's team found that the respondents proceeded through the stages in the predicted order and that there were no examples of individuals going backwards to a previous stage (Colby *et al* 1983).

While Kohlberg's views have been widely supported they have also been criticized, as have all stage theories. Theoreticians who support the idea that moral development is stage-like have tended to criticize the details of Kohlberg's descriptions of progression towards moral justice, many claiming that there are more, or different, stages. Critics of the model point out that individuals respond to different dilemmas in different ways. So a person cannot be said to be at any single level of cognitive development.

Cultural and gender differences

Two criticisms in particular have been raised. The first concerns cultural differences. In cultures which emphasize the importance of collective responsibility few individuals, if any, reach stages 5 or 6. In Israel, for example, the kibbutz communities are organized by shared living arrangements and practices. Research has found that members of kibbutzim refuse to accept that the druggist has the right to decide who gets the drug. In other words, in some cultures people may develop moral codes which simply differ from that proposed as being preferable, according to Kohlberg's model.

The second criticism has come from one of Kohlberg's research associates, Carol Gilligan, who published a book in 1982 entitled *In a Different Voice: Psychological Theory and Women's Development*. In keeping with the criticism that Kohlberg's views are bounded by his own cultural perspective, Gilligan argues that his theory is biased towards a male view of the world – in short, it is sexist. Her claim is that men and women have different viewpoints which influence their moral values. She argues that the sequence of stages proposed by Kohlberg reflects a male bias towards detachment and notions of rights and obligations which reflect this. In contrast, she argues, women are more concerned about relationships. Their moral code is much more focused upon the care of others rather than abstract notions of justice. Gilligan studied the difficult judgments which women make in real life when deciding whether or not to have an abortion. She found that young women were much more concerned about people and their feelings than the sorts of principles that Kohlberg describes in his model. Gilligan used these women's judgments to devise a new theory of moral development based upon a commitment to people, not principles. Whether or not men and women do have different moral codes, Gilligan's analysis has revealed that Kohlberg's model reflects only one system of thought and conduct. Now that moral relativism is on the agenda, the force of Kohlberg's analysis is open to question.

SAQ
22

Outline briefly Kohlberg's model of moral development. What are the major criticisms?

Conclusion

Moral development is a good example of a stage theory in development. The issue of moral development is also important because psychologists are often asked to contribute to the social policy debate about public conduct, particularly the problems of youth culture. In many respects society expects too much of psychologists in terms of what we can discover. We know that in the right circumstances children and adults will perform an immoral act such as stealing or cheating if they think they will get away with it – this has been tested repeatedly in experiments. Yet developmental psychologists like Piaget and Kohlberg stress that the critical issue is the individual's understanding of the complexities of justice and responsibility. Kohlberg's model may be culture-specific, unclear in parts and a male view of morality; however, it shows how intricate are the moral decisions which we face, and the large amount of available data do conform to the pattern of stages which he predicts.

Summary

❒ Research techniques examining infant perception reveal the value of inventive experimental procedures.

❒ We can define what play is but are as yet unclear about its role in development.

❒ Theories of moral development illustrate the uses and criticisms of stage theories.

Conclusion: Development in a life-span perspective

This Unit has discussed many topics and it is necessary to draw the strands together in this concluding part. As Part 1 and Figure 1 show, developmental psychology addresses questions which have been raised for a variety of different historical reasons, ranging from evolutionary questions about how we develop as a species, to pressing social questions of the day. This diversity is brought together partly by the sophisticated technology and methods used within the discipline, particularly the use of longitudinal research designs where the same individuals are studied over a period of time. The discussion in Part 5, on the technology for studying infant perception, illustrates the technological sophistication required to study development, especially in very young children.

What is development?

What do we understand by the term 'development'? Part 2 of the Unit attempted to show that accounts of development based upon environmental or maturational explanations have been considered by developmental psychologists to be somewhat circular. In studying how our genes and the environment *interact*, it is held that we need to envisage how the individual *constructs* an understanding of his or her experiences of objects in the physical world and social relationships. Developmental theories thus tend to argue that people's understanding changes in stage-like ways, shifting from one way of construing events to another in ways as revolutionary as the change in the butterfly's metamorphosis.

The example of stages discussed in Part 5 was Kohlberg's model of how moral development from the primary school years into adulthood is characterized by increasingly complex ways of understanding the pros and cons of any dilemma. The analysis of the evidence cited to support Kohlberg's theory suggested that stage models are interesting but are hard to support with clear experimental evidence.

Part 3 argued that the evidence on phylogenic comparisons between our own and other species suggest that there seem to be clear differences between ourselves and our nearest evolutionary relatives. The higher-order primates seem capable of simple tasks like deception and basic communication. We see in the different calls that vervet monkeys make to one another in the event of danger, that some elements of language are present. However, it is still fair to suggest that our own species is endowed with these abilities in such greater abundance that even a pre-school child can reflect upon the nature of these skills themselves. By reflecting upon their relationships and their communication with others such children are demonstrating that one of the fundamental human attributes is that we are all 'folk psychologists'. Such skills seem to be uniquely human.

Part 4 examined the methods used in developmental psychology. All of these – experiment, observation and interview – are used elsewhere in psychology. However, developmentalists use them in order to grasp how *change* occurs in individuals. Cross-sectional studies are very widely used but this is largely because they are cheap and easy to conduct. Longitudinal studies and those with a training phase are truly developmental; but, as the example of play and learning in Part 5 suggested, interpreting these studies is not without problems.

Fitting the pieces together: the life-span approach

How can we tie all the strands of developmental psychology together? Over the past twenty years we have become increasingly aware of the complexities of the possible influences upon us. We look less for single determinants of change in individuals and more for the combination of factors which appear to reveal the differences between individuals who share the same genetic make-up or social background. The German developmentalist, Paul Baltes (Baltes and Schaie, 1973), has done much to herald this change. He points out that developmental psychology needs to take into account two factors which it has tended to neglect.

The first is that development is for life, not just a feature of childhood. It is true that great change occurs in childhood, particularly in intellectual and language development (e.g. see Figure 11), but we would be mistaken to assume that change does not occur in adulthood. Intellectual change does take place, as we saw in the discussion of Kohlberg's model in Part 5. Raymond Catell (1971) has long argued that just as speed of thinking declines from the late twenties, so 'wisdom', the ability to understand all sides of an argument, may increase as an adult matures. Some of the changes which Baltes discusses, like the menopause or ageing, are biological. Others, such as the tendency for teenagers to go to university after school or for individuals to retire at 65, are culturally specified. All these pressures on what an individual does are what Baltes calls **'normative age-graded'** influences.

The influence of 'history'

The second issue raised by Baltes is that historical events influence us. He stressed that normative age-graded experiences do not occur in a vacuum. Rather they unfold within events that either influence all members of a generation or within the complex web of an individual experience. So 'history' is experienced in two ways. Firstly, there are what he calls **'normative history-graded'** influences. These can be biological as we see in the relationship between better nutrition over the past century and the lowering in the age of puberty, for example. They can also be culturally determined, like the influence of war upon the population of Bosnia through the 1990s. Influences can also affect individuals, not only whole generations. These Baltes calls **'non-normative life events'**. They include biological factors like the brain damage caused by genetic effects such as Down's syndrome or the influence of a severe car accident. There are also social non-normative events, such as the effects of a particular divorce upon a child.

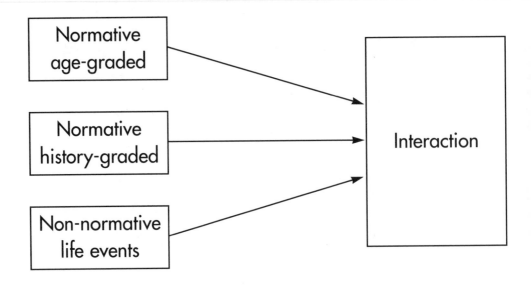

FIGURE 35 : *Baltes' model of development.*

Figure 35 shows how the components of Baltes' model fit together. The three influences on development (normative age-graded, normative history-graded and non-normative life events) are each the product of biological and environmental determinants, particularly the interaction between the two (see Figure 8). They interact with one another over time to influence the development of the individual. Each of us shares some characteristics with all others, such as the experience of universal life-changes (e.g. puberty, or the need to acquire the intellectual skills required for understanding moral rules), some components of our make-up which are common to our generation or culture (like being a school-leaver at a time of high unemployment, or a member of a war-torn culture); and also some characteristics which are unique to our individual circumstances and life histories. It is the task of developmental psychology to discern the relative contributions of each of these components.

SAQ
23

Define briefly the three components of Baltes' model of life-span development.

FURTHER READING

BREMNER, J. G. (1994) *Infancy* [second edn]. Oxford: Basil Blackwell.
LLOYD, P. (1995) *Cognitive and Language Development.* Leicester: BPS Books, Open Learning Unit.
SCHAFFER, H. R. (1995) *Early Socialization.* Leicester: BPS Books, Open Learning Unit.
SMITH, P. K. and COWIE, H. (1991) *Understanding Children's Development* [second edn]. Oxford: Basil Blackwell.
TUCKER, N. (1996) *Adolescence, Adulthood and Ageing.* Leicester: BPS Books, Open Learning Unit.
TURNER, P. (1995) *Sex, Gender and Identity.* Leicester: BPS Books, Open Learning Unit.

REFERENCES

ANTELL, S. E. and KEATING, D. P. (1983) Perception of numerical invariance in neonates. *Child Development*, 54, 695 – 701.

BALTES, P. and SCHAIE, L. (1973) *Life-span Developmental Psychology*. London: Academic Press.

BANDURA, A. (1971) *Psychological Modelling*. Chicago: Aldine.

BAUMRIND, D. (1971) Current patterns of parental authority. *Developmental Psychology Monographs*, 4.

BRONFENBRENNER, U. (1979) *The Ecology of Human Development*. Cambridge, Mass: Harvard University Press.

BROWN, R. (1973) A *First Language*. Cambridge, Mass: Harvard University Press.

CAREY, S. (1985) *Conceptual Change in Childhood*. Cambridge, Mass: MIT Press.

CARRAHER, T. N., CARRAHER, D.W. & SCHLIEMAN, A. D. (1985) Mathematics in the Streets and in Schools. *British Journal of Developmental Psychology*, 3, 21 – 29.

CATTELL, R. B. (1971) *Abilities: Their Structure, Growth and Action*. Boston: Houghton Mifflin

CHENEY, D. L. & SEYFARTH, R. M. (1990) *How Monkeys see the World*. Chicago: Chicago Unversity Press.

CHERLIN, A. J. *et al*. (1991) Longitudinal studies of effects of divorce on children in Great Britain and the United States. *Science*, 252, 1386 – 1389.

CHOMSKY, N. (1957) *Syntactic Structures*. The Hague: Mouton.

COLBY, A. KOHLBERG, L., GIBBS, J. and LIEBERMAN, M (1983) A longitudinal study of moral development. *Monographs of the Society of Research in Child Development*, 48.

DUNN, J. (1988) *The Beginnings of Social Understanding*. Oxford: Basil Blackwell.

GILLIGAN, C. (1982) *In a Different Voice: Psychological Theory and Women's Development*. Cambridge, Mass: Harvard University Press.

HARPER, L. V. and HUIE, K. S. (1985) The effects of prior group experience, age and familiarity on the quality and organization of preschoolers' social relationships. *Child Development*, 56, 704 – 717.

HUMPHREY, N. (1976) The social function of the intellect. in P. P. G. Bateson & R. A. Hinde |Eds| *Growing Points of Ethology*. Cambridge: Cambridge University Press.

KRASNOR, L and PEPLER, D. J. (1980) The study of children's play: Some suggested future directions. in K. H. Rubin |Ed.| *Children's Play*. San Francisco: Jossey-Bass

LIEBERT, R. M. and SPRAFKIN, J. (1988) *The Early Window*. Oxford: Pergamon.

PARTEN, M. (1932) Social participation among preschool children. *Journal of Abnormal and Social Psychology*, 27, 243 – 269.

PIAGET, J. (1932) *The Moral Judgement of the Child*. London:Penguin (re-issued 1977).

PIAGET, J. (1953) *The Origin of Intelligence in the Child*. London: Routledge and Kegan Paul.

POVINELLI, D. J. and EDDY, T. J. (1994) The eyes as a window: What chimpanzees see on the other side. *Current Psychology of Cognition*, 13, 695 – 705.

PREMACK, D. (1971) Language in chimpanzees? *Science*, 172, 808 – 822.

SLATER, A., MORISON, V., TOWN, C. & ROSE, D. (1985) Movement perception and identity constancy in the newborn baby. *British Journal of Developmental Psychology*, 3, 211 – 220.

SIMON, T. and SMITH, P.K. (1984) Object play, problem solving and creativity in children. In P. K. Smith |Ed.| *Play: in Animals and Humans*. Oxford: Basil Blackwell.

SMITH, P. K. and VOLLSTEDT, R. (1985) On defining play: an empirical study of the relationship between play and various play criteria. *Child Development*, 56, 1042 – 1050.

SODIAN, B. (1994) Early deception and the conceptual continuity claim. In C. Lewis & P. Mitchell (Ed) *Children's Early Understanding of Mind*. Hove: Erlbaum (Taylor and Francis) UK.

SUTTON-SMITH, B. and KELLY-BYRNE, D. (1984) The idealization of play. In P. K. Smith |Ed.| *Play: in Animals and Humans*. Oxford: Basil Blackwell.

SYLVA, K. (1977) Play and learning. In B. Tizard & D. Harvey |Eds| *The Biology of Play*. London: SIMP/ Heinemann.

TREVARTHEN, C. (1977) Descriptive analysis of infant communicative behaviour. In H. R. Schaffer |Ed.| *Studies of Mother – infant interaction*. London: Academic Press.

WHITEN, A and BYRNE, R. W. (1988) Tactical deception in primates. *Behavioural and Brain Sciences*, 11, 233 – 273.

ANSWERS TO SELF-ASSESSMENT QUESTIONS

SAQ 1

Statement	Perspective
Boys will be boys	Nature
Some leaders are born great	Nature
'I'm depraved on account of being deprived'	Nurture
Some leaders have greatness thrust upon them	Nurture
Ryan Giggs is an instinctive footballer	Nature

SAQ 2 There are at least three ways in which Darwin has influenced the ways in which children have been studied:

(1) his methods of close observation of a species' behaviour;

(2) The theory of evolution describes the development of *Homo sapiens* (you and me) as a species that has much in common with other related species;

(3) his diary study of his son.

SAQ 3 By and large the hygienist approach sides with the nurture perspective as it stresses the need to impose order in the child's life. The permissive approach is more naturist, following the assumptions of the French philosopher Jean Jacques Rousseau (1712 – 1778) that people are born with inherent goodness that can be damaged by corrupting influences.

SAQ 4 The layers are:

(1) *Microsystem*: a set of relationships, like a family or within a nursery school.

(2) *Mesosystem*: the link between different sets of relationships, such as those between home and school.

(3) *Exosystem*: the way in which a local community organizes what people do. Some, for example, run well-equipped nurseries with professionally trained staff, while others leave the care of the pre-schoolers to whatever parents can organize.

(4) *Macrosystem*: this refers to the way in which a culture as a whole organizes itself. For example, the shift from hygienism to permissiveness (discussed in SAQ 3) reflects a change in the macrosystem.

SAQ 5 The major differences between models of continuity versus discontinuity are:

continuity	discontinuity
continuous growth	stage-like or qualitative skills
gradual change	rapid change
piecemeal change	complete or holistic change simultaneity

SAQ 6 Social learning theory is squarely within the tradition which assumes that development is a *continuous* process whereby the acquisition of 'behaviour' involves the gradual development of, and change in, particular skills.

SAQ7 This is something of a trick question because there is no single or straightforward answer – though hopefully it made you think! When considering certain attributes such as intelligence or personality, maturation theorists tend to

assume continuity – we are constrained by our inborn capabilities. However, when it comes to other skills, such as learning to walk or talk, change can be rapid and discontinuous.

SAQ 8 Genotype _____ Environment

maturation Piaget Vygotsky Bronfenbrenner social learning theory behaviourism

SAQ 9 The two main features of human language are that it contains spontaneous, novel communicative patterns and that it is not literal – it refers to more abstract concepts than simpler, primate communication systems. However, you might have thought of other features of language that are not mentioned in the Unit. For example, it contains a complex grammatical structure known as a syntax. Secondly, it contains a flexibility as a result of not necessarily being literal. Metaphor, the use of a word or phrase to convey two meanings, is one such flexibility. Primate communication is much simpler and more literal.

SAQ 10 Age usually refers to chronological age – how old a child is. The term 'stage' applies to a level of competence or development. So, for example, an individual who has reached puberty becomes an adolescent. Age and stage are related to one another, but may not overlap completely; for example, some individuals reach puberty at age 11 while others may not do so until four years later.

SAQ 11 The three main features of Piaget's approaches are:

- detailed observation of how children tackle individual problems
- simple, yet revealing tasks which show stage-like shifts in performance
- reflexive questioning in which the depth of understanding is explored.

SAQ 12

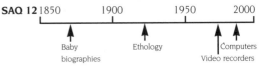

SAQ 13 The main advantage of experimental studies is that they allow the researcher to manipulate the relative influence of possible contributory factors. Other factors are that they are relatively efficient of time and money and they allow the experimenter to control events.

SAQ 14 *Problems with observational studies*: these include

- lack of control
- not being able to tease apart cause and effect
- 'observer effects'
- competence/performance distinctions.

Problems with experimental methods: these include

- artificiality arising from manipulating or controlling events
- unfamiliarity of laboratory settings
- experimenter effects and producing results that might not reflect true competence.

SAQ 15 Interviews can be used to probe respondents' knowledge or attitudes, to examine their naïve 'theories', to examine broader or ecological influences upon individuals.

SAQ 16 Three main methods used in developmental psychology:

(i) *The cross sectional study*: its main advantage is that it allows quick and easy comparisons, for example between different age groups. It is also cheap. Its disadvantage is that it demonstrates differences between groups but not the processes or mechanisms of change or development.

(ii) *The longitudinal study*: the advantage is that this method is truly developmental, in that it charts the changes occurring within the same individuals over time. This allows us to tease apart the possible influences on such change. However it is necessarily more costly in terms of time and money.

(iii) *The intervention study*: allows experimenters both the control over what they study and the advantage of examining change within the same individuals. The disadvantage is that the change effected by the researchers may be artificial.

SAQ 17 Spontaneous preference and the habituation – dishabituation (habituation – novelty) procedures have been most commonly used to study the perceptual skills of newborn children. These techniques show whether young infants discriminate between different shapes (like crosses, circles and scambled faces), numbers of dots, and different orientations. Two further techniques examine either the eye movements or retinas of infants as they observe a stimulus. These allow researchers to explore how infants scan an array and how well they focus.

SAQ 18 The two predominant views of play that we inherited from nineteenth analyses were (1) that it is an expression of 'surplus' energy and (2) that it is a means of practising skills in a safe setting. Cognitive approaches such as Piaget's and Bruner's fit the second category. A third category, play as a means of addressing unconscious feelings, has been put forward by psychoanalysts.

SAQ 19 I would classify the games as follows, but you might have good reason to devise a different classification system.

chess	game with rules
cops and robbers	rough and tumble, plus ritual play
'tig' or 'tag'	rough and tumble
making up rhymes	ritual play
netball	game with rules
wendy house cooking	symbolic play
grandmother's footsteps	game with rules, often turning into rough and tumble
Simon says	game with rules
answering an SAQ	a game with rules? or ritual rehearsal?

SAQ 20 Krasnor and Pepler's criteria are:
(1) rough and tumble;
(2) symbolic play;
(3) ritual play;
(4) games with rules.
The main way of assessing whether these criteria define play is to see if different observers classify the same act of play in the same way, as Smith and Vollstedt (1985) did.

SAQ 21 Sutton-Smith and Kelly-Byrne's claim is that we have assumed that human play is a purely biological phenomenon. Yet in reality (they argue) how we perceive play is largely a reflection of our philosophical and cultural views about childhood. In particular, they point out that the association between what children do and the term 'play' was made by social policy commentators as a result of a 'youth' problem in the late nineteenth century. Figure 1 depicts all the influences on our understanding.

SAQ 22 Kohlberg's model claims that adolescents and young adults develop an increasingly complex understanding of morality and that changes appear to be stage-like. The shifts occur between levels from pre-conventional to conventional to post-conventional. The two main criticisms have focused upon the basis of the theory in favour of one cultural group (that of North American culture) and one sex (men).

SAQ 23 As Figure 12 shows, the three components are:

(1) *normative age-graded influences*: the effects of life experiences which occur either as a result of our biological maturation (e.g. puberty) or as a result of cultural norms (e.g. going to school at age 5).

(2) *normative history-graded influences*: the effects of historical change upon us as shown up in generational changes. These might be biological (e.g. the lowering in the age of puberty over the past century) or social (e.g. raising the minimum age of school leavers from 14 to 16 since the Second World War).

(3) *non-normative life events*: life experiences which do not occur to whole populations (e.g. being injured in a car crash) which nevertheless influence the course of development.

GLOSSARY

Authoritarian parenting: a style which emphasizes obedience and favours punishment as a way of making the child compliant.

authoritative parenting: a style which involves explaining rules to children and listening to children's points of view, even if such opinions are not accepted. The aim is to make the child independent.

autonomous morality (see *internal morality*)

behaviour modification: the gradual change of behaviour by a system of graded rewards. Used in treating individuals with problems and based upon Learning Theory.

blind trial: a procedure to reduce testing bias. The researcher is not aware of which grouping the participant is in.

cohort study: study of a group identified by age. The term usually applies to a large scale investigation (e.g. all the children born in the UK within one week, over many years).

competence–performance distinction: the idea that how individuals perform (for example in a test or experiment) may not display what they are capable of.

constructivist perspective: the belief that psychological development is not simply the product of environmental and biological forces. Rather it consists of the individual coming to make his or her own interpretations of events. Such interptretations are thought to change in a stage-like way.

conventional moral reasoning: according to Kohlberg's theory this approach is based largely upon the acceptance of prescribed rules.

cross sectional study: a study of two different populations. In developmental psychology the usual comparison is between different age groups.

dishabituation: a renewal of attention, once a stimulus is changed.

empiricist: someone who believes that knowledge is reliably derived only from direct observation.

ethology: the study of animal behaviour and its place in evolution, using observational procedures.

exosystem: part of Bronfenbrenner's Ecological Model referring to a set of social institutions, such as local government institutions, which influence individuals but in which they are not directly involved.

external morality: an unquestioning obedience to rules set by more powerful individuals – usually parents. Contrasts with internal morality.

field experiment: a study which is conducted outside the laboratory and which makes use of a naturally-occurring event, such as children going to a new school. Usually, participants are naturally allocated to groups (e.g. different classes).

genotype: the total set of genes that an individual inherits.

habituation: the gradual decrease in attention to a particular stimulus. Used in studying babies' perceptual discrimination.

heteronomous morality: see *external morality*.

holism: the belief that one area of psychological functioning necessarily influences others. Assumed in some constructivist theories.

hygienism: the name given to the philosophy of child care in a 'scientific' or 'hygienic' manner, popular in the 1920s, but still influential.

innate: an influence upon psychological functioning which is inborn, or genetically determined, over and above any influences of the environment.

inner (or internal) working model: the belief system that individuals hold about themselves which develops from the security of their attachment relationships.

instinct: an inborn (see *innate*) ability to perform and act without consciously reflecting upon doing so.

instrumental-exchange: an approach to moral reasoning by which, according to Kohlberg's theory, children at the pre-conventional level appear to see both sides of a moral issue but think only in terms of the gains and losses and not about the moral principles.

internal morality: a morality which assumes that rules are arbitrary and agreed upon. Contrasts with external morality.

law-and-order: a stage of Kohlberg's theory of moral development at which individuals stress the overlap between society's rules and those held by individuals and the family.

linear development: growth in the individual which occurs in an additive fashion without obvious changes in its nature.

macrosystem: Bronfenbrenner's term for 'culture'. In other words, the sets of beliefs, values and laws that regulate the conduct of a member of a society.

maturation: developmental change which is directed by hereditary (i.e. genetic) mechanisms.

mesosystem: according to Bronfenbrenner's Ecological Model (see Figure 2) this level of social organization is the relationship between the individual's different environmental settings. The demands of a social life at college versus parents' expectations of a student's academic success are but one example of such links.

metamorphosis: change from one form to another (e.g. from pupa to butterfly).

microsystem: the immediate interactions of an individual, for example, in a family.

nativism: the belief that behavioural repertoires and their development are controlled by hereditary (i.e. genetic) influences.

natural experiment: see *field experiment*.

nature: see *nativism*.

non-normative life event: an unexpected event which occurs to a small section of the population, which influences the course of those individuals' development. Such events vary from biological traumas, such as having Down's syndrome, to social experiences, like being caught up in a war.

normative age-graded influences: influences upon us which occur naturally occur in all members of our species, such as the ability to walk, or puberty.

normative history-graded influences: influences which change over the course of history, such as lower fertility rates caused by environmental pollution.

nurture: see *nativism*

ontogeny: the development of the individual from conception to death.